Coaching Synchronized Swimming Effectively

Margaret Swan Forbes
M.Ed., Trinity University

with contributions by

Donald T. Kane
Dawn Bean
and
United States Synchronized Swimming Staff

This is a publication for

The United States Synchronized Swimming's
National Achievement Program

and

American Coaching Effectiveness Program
Level I Synchronized Swimming

Human Kinetics Publishers, Inc.
Champaign, Illinois 61820

Library of Congress Cataloging in Publication Data

Forbes, Margaret Swan.
   Coaching synchronized swimming effectively.

   Bibliography: p.
   1. Synchronized swimming—Coaching. I. Kane,
Donald T. II. Bean, Dawn. III. Title.
GV838.53.S95F67   1984   797.2'1   84-15853
ISBN 0-931250-80-3

Production Director: John Keith Foster
Developmental Editor: Fran Rivkin
Copy Editor: Tim Bryant
Typesetter: Carol McCarty
Text Layout: Lezli Harris
Illustrator: Karen Crabtree Hertzler
Cover Design and Layout: The Design Group, Inc.

ISBN: 0-931250-80-3

Copyright © 1984 by United States Synchronized Swimming

All rights reserved. Except for use in a review, the reproduction or utilization of this work in any form or by any electronic, mechanical, or other means, now known or hereafter invented, including xerography, photocopying and recording, and in any information retrieval system, is forbidden without the written permission of the publisher.

Printed in the United States of America

10 9 8 7 6 5 4 3 2

Human Kinetics Publishers, Inc.
Box 5076, Champaign, IL 61820

CONTENTS

PREFACE	vii
INTRODUCTION AND GLOSSARIES	1
The Skills	2
Swimming Sequences	2
Curriculum Overview	5
The Language of Synchro	7
UNIT I	17
Side Stroke	18
Crawl Stroke	20
Eel (Standard Scull)	22
Snail (Reverse Standard Scull)	24
Tub	26

Somersault, Back Tuck	27
Oyster	29
Water Wheel	30
Sequence 1	32

UNIT II — 35

Back Stroke	36
Breast Stroke	38
Canoe Scull	40
Alligator Scull	42
Torpedo Scull	44
Corkscrew	47
Log Roll	48
Somersault, Front Pike	50
Jumpover	52
Sequence 2	53

UNIT III — 55

Side Flutter Kick and Variations	56
Reverse Torpedo Scull	57
Bent Knee Position Scull, Supine	59
Bent Knee Position Scull, Prone	61
Shark Circle	63
Marlin	65
Somersault, Back Pike	67
Dolphin, Head-First	69
Sequence 3	71

UNIT IV — 73

Eggbeater Kick, Stationary	74
Lobster Scull	76
Vertical Tuck Position	78
Inverted Split Position with Support Scull	80
Ballet Leg, Single and Alternate	83
Walkover, Front	85

Dolphin, Bent Knee	87
Porpoise	88
Sequence 4	90

UNIT V — 91

Eggbeater Kick, Traveling	92
Flamingo Position	93
Crane Position	94
Ballet Leg Submarine, Single	96
Somersub	98
Walkover, Back	100
Barracuda	102
Sequence 5	104

UNIT VI — 105

Transitions	106
Inverted Vertical Position with Support Scull Hold	106
Inverted Split Rotation	108
Kip	110
Eiffel Walk	112
Swordfish	114
Dolphin, Foot-First	116
Sequence 6	118

APPENDICES — 119

Appendix A: Scull Chart	121
Appendix B: National Achievement Program Requirements	123

BIBLIOGRAPHY — 126

PREFACE

Resembling scenes from an old Esther Williams movie, swimmers across the nation can be seen gliding through the water to accompanying music. With their legs held high and their arms gracefully extended, synchronized swimmers are now capturing American's attention with a sport that has evolved from the MGM spectaculars into a highly competitive Olympic sport. Its renewed popularity can be attributed to the enjoyment, beauty, and challenge of synchronized swimming.

People of all ages and aspirations enjoy synchronized swimming—from those who just want to have fun to those who dream of being in the Olympics. Whether you're teaching a beginner's class or training swimmers for competition, the more knowledge you have about synchronized swimming, the more effective a teacher or coach you will be. *Coaching Synchronized Swimming Effectively* is an essential resource for aquatics instructors who hope to or already are coaching synchronized swimming, whether it be with the American Red Cross, the YMCA, the YWCA, parks and recreation departments, or elementary, secondary, or college physical education programs.

This manual will help you teach the basic synchro skills needed to compete in sanctioned U.S. Synchronized Swimming Novice, Age Group, Junior Olympic, College, and Masters competition. *Coaching Synchronized Swimming Effectively* begins with the most elementary skills and progresses to the more complex. Each skill is presented clearly and logically.

The ideas in this manual were first compiled in 1980 in conjunction with U.S. Synchronized Swimming under the direction of its president, Judith S. McGowan. The manual has been developed further by Kim E. Van Buskirk. An early version was distributed to coaches, both novice and experienced, whose insights served to expand and update this "bible" on basic synchronized swimming. Special thanks go to the Lilly Endowment for helping to offset the costs of the manual with a grant.

Margaret Swan Forbes
Retired Professor
Department of Physical Education
San Antonio College

U.S. SYNCHRONIZED SWIMMING

Coaching Synchronized Swimming Effectively serves as the official text of the U.S. Synchronized Swimming's National Coaches Certification Program. U.S. Synchronized Swimming, better known as Synchro-USA, is responsible for the education and training of athletes, coaches, judges, and officials on all levels of competition. This organization fields the championship teams that represent the U.S. in international competition, including the Olympic Games. Synchro-USA is recognized by the International Olympic Committee, the U.S. Olympic Committee, and FINA, the International Aquatic Federation.

Members of Synchro-USA receive a bimonthly newsletter which focuses on current issues and reports on the most current developments in the sport and in educational resources. Members also receive insurance benefits and more. For further information, contact the national headquarters in Indianapolis—Synchro-USA, 901 W. New York St., Indianapolis, IN 46223 (phone 317 633-2000).

INTRODUCTION AND GLOSSARIES

Synchronized swimming, or "synchro," is a combination of rhythmic swimming and gymnastics performed in the water, all set to music. Imagine a gymnast performing underwater or an ice skater perfecting her figures in an unstable medium. The synchronized swimmer performs many movements which resemble the skills performed by the gymnast or figure skater, and then choreographs them into a routine using a dancer's artistic flair, all while in the water. As in dancing, figure skating, and gymnastics, the synchronized swimmer must perform skills which demand tremendous strength and endurance, with the grace and style to make the intricate maneuvers look effortless.

The synchronized swimmer takes various figures and positions, and combines them through the use of seemingly effortless transitions. These combinations are performed in time to accompanying music. This manual will help you coach synchronized swimming. It includes well-illustrated, complete instructions for teaching all the beginning-level figures, positions, and transitions.

The manual is organized into six units. Skills presented in later units, or even later within a unit often build on skills presented earlier. Thus, it is a good idea to teach the skills in the order in which they are presented. It is possible to skip around some, but you should make sure that the more advanced skill doesn't build on a skill the swimmer hasn't learned.

Each skill is presented in the same way. The presentation starts with an illustration of the skill. Unless marked otherwise, all skills run from left to right. Examine each illustration carefully. Coaches need a clear mental image of a skill to teach it well. With several of the skills, the illustration is followed by a brief section which highlights the position of major body parts. Then the method of execution is described, along with a step-by-step approach for teaching the skill. The discussion of each skill concludes with a list of the mistakes swimmers make most often while learning the skill and a corresponding list of ways to correct the mistakes. Interspersed within the text are "Coaching Tips" which can help coaches communicate various aspects of the skills.

The Skills

The skills of each unit are divided into three major categories: (a) strokes and transitions, (b) basic positions and sculls, and (c) figures.

Strokes and Transitions

Strokes and transitions move the swimmer from one body position or figure to another, and from one place to another in the pool. Most strokes are adapted from traditional swimming strokes, usually by keeping the head out of the water. To perform the strokes and transitions of synchronized swimming, swimmers should be able to perform the fundamentals of the traditional strokes. The material presented here should be a review of the traditional strokes, and an explanation of any modifications of these strokes for synchro.

Basic Positions and Sculls

Basic positions are the foundation of the figures. The basic body positions are described on pages 10-15. Sculling is a movement in which the hands and arms apply continuous pressure against the water to support, balance, and/or propel the body. Appendix A contains a Scull chart which includes the body position, hand position, wrist position, and direction of movement for each scull.

Figures

Figures are movements in the water composed of one or more of the basic body positions. For example, a figure may involve getting into one position and rotating, or it may involve moving from one position into another.

Swimming Sequences

Each unit concludes with a synchronized swimming sequence. A sequence is a choreographed routine of individual skills combined in a logical pattern. Within this routine the swimmer moves smoothly through the water in time to music. Swimmers should strive to execute precise and controlled movements in their sequences. The sequence at the end of each unit is a combination of the skills learned in that unit, plus previously learned skills. Five components of sequences—pool pattern, variety, creativity, presentation, and swimming to music—are briefly discussed below.

Pool Pattern

The pool pattern is the path of the swimmer as she performs the sequence. Swimmers should use almost the entire pool in a logical progression of angular, straight, and broken lines. The physical limitations of the pool must be considered in the planning of a pattern. For example, swimmers should only perform vertical descents when they are in the deep end so that the vertical line of the body isn't broken.

The pool pattern of the sequences described in this manual will vary slightly among swimmers. For example, as swimmers become more skilled, their strokes become more powerful and each stroke propels them further. If a swimmer reaches the side of the pool during a sequence, she obviously will have to change direction in order to continue. The differing dimensions of pools will also affect the pool pattern, since it takes fewer strokes to cross a 15-yard pool than a 25-yard pool.

Variety

Variety is the spice of a swimming sequence. Swimmers should include different strokes and methods of propulsion, different types of figures within the sequence, and different directions of movement. As swimmers learn more and more skills, they will be able to add to the variety of their routines.

Creativity

Creating one's own swimming sequences is part of the fun of synchronized swimming. Encourage swimmers to start choreographing their own routines as soon as possible. Swimmers enjoy creating their own sequences, and it is good practice for them for later units.

Presentation

Presence and style are also important components of the swimming sequence. As a swimmer progresses, she will become more and more confident and will present herself with poise. A swimmer should strive to make the sequence look as if it were effortless. As with most sports, the better the athlete, the harder the skills she can perform, and the easier it looks.

Swimming to Music

Movement in the water synchronized to music is the foundation of synchronized swimming. The choreography of the sequence should paint a visual picture of the music. Music should be incorporated into almost all practices so swimmers will understand it to be an integral part of the sport. Swimmers also tend to enjoy the sport more when music is added.

To swim to music, the swimmer must have a basic understanding of music structure. Music is divided into measures, each of which has a certain number of beats. The number of beats, or counts, in a measure is called the "time" of the music. The time of a piece is on the left of the first line of a written piece of music. Most American music is written in 4/4 time. The first number means that there are four beats in a measure. If the time is 3/4, there are three beats in each measure.

The second number indicates what kind of note is one beat in the measure. In the case of 4/4 time, it is a quarter note. It isn't necessary to know this number to be able to count to the music.

In music, basic themes are organized into patterns. Most American music is based on themes which run for four measures. The "Syncopated Clock" is the music for the sequence in the first unit. It is a good example of a piece in 4/4 time which has two themes. Listen to it several times until you can hum the whole piece.

A music chart is a useful tool for choreographing swimming movements. Instead of using the music written out in notes, you use only the beats and measures of the music. A chart has been constructed below for the "Syncopated Clock." The measures are organized in rows, and the beats are organized in columns. The themes are grouped together also.

Once you have the music written in chart form, you can note the movements which occur at each point in the music on the chart. For example, the first four measures may look like the following chart for Sequence 1.

"Syncopated Clock" Notation

Measures	Beats:	1	2	3	4	Theme
X		/	/	/	/	Intro
X		/	/	/	/	
1		/	/	/	/	A
2		/	/	/	/	
3		/	/	/	/	
4		/	/	/	/	
5		/	/	/	/	A
6		/	/	/	/	
7		/	/	/	/	
8		/	/	/	/	
9		/	/	/	/	B
10		/	/	/	/	
11		/	/	/	/	
12		/	/	/	/	
13		/	/	/	/	A
14		/	/	/	/	
15		/	/	/	/	
16		/	/	/	/	

SEQUENCE 1
Music: Syncopated Clock by Leroy Anderson

Measures	Beats 1	2	3	4
1	Right side scissors kick	Left arm Crawl	Left side scissors kick	Right arm Crawl
2	Right side scissors kick	Left arm Crawl	Left side scissors kick	Right arm Crawl
3	Right Side Stroke	Glide	Right Side Stroke	Roll on to back on right arm
4	Eel scull, traveling	⟶		Eel scull, stationary

There is more to music than beats and measures. The charts should become more specific as you become more familiar with listening to music. You can note accent points, changes in the volume of the music, high notes, low notes, powerful sections, abrupt changes, or anything else which might affect the swimmer's interpretation of the music. The swimmer must learn to perform her movements so that they enhance and complement the mood of the music.

Curriculum Overview

Listed below is a chart of the entire curriculum of the Level I Program that comprises this manual. With this chart you can see exactly which skills are part of which unit, and how the skills build on one another.

LEVEL I CURRICULUM

Unit	Strokes and Transitions	Sculls and Basic Positions	Figures	Music for Sequences
1	Side Stroke Crawl Stroke	Eel (Standard Scull) Snail (Reverse Standard Scull)	Tub Somersault, Back Tuck Oyster Water Wheel	"Syncopated Clock"

Level I Curriculum (cont.)

2	Back Stroke Breast Stroke	Canoe Alligator Torpedo	Corkscrew Log Roll Somersault, Front Pike Jumpover	"California Girls"
3	Side Flutter and Variations	Reverse Torpedo Bent Knee, Supine Bent Knee, Prone	Shark Circle Marlin Somersault, Back Pike Dolphin, Head-First	"Lemon Tree"
4	Eggbeater Kick, Stationary	Lobster Vertical Tuck Inverted Split with Support Scull	Ballet Leg, Single and Alternate Walkover, Front Dolphin, Bent Knee Porpoise	"Fiddler On The Roof"
5	Eggbeater Kick, Traveling	Flamingo Crane	Ballet Leg Submarine, Single Somersub Walkover, Back Barracuda	"Yellow Rose of Texas"
6	Transitions Created By Swimmer	Inverted Vertical with Support Scull Hold Inverted Split Rotation	Kip Eiffel Walk Swordfish Dolphin, Foot-First	Swimmer's Own Selection

The Language of Synchro

A special language is needed in synchronized swimming to describe all of the figures, body positions, and transitions. The remainder of this introduction describes the language of synchronized swimming. The "Lingo" section is a glossary of terms frequently used to explain synchro movements. The following section is a glossary of body positions. It is a good idea to go through these glossaries before reading the descriptions of the skills. The more familiar you are with these terms and body positions, the easier the skill explanations will be to understand. You will probably find yourself referring back to the glossaries as you go through the skills.

Lingo

The following terms refer to the relation of parts of the body to other parts, or the relation of the body to the water.

Arch—To bend the body backward so that the back and hips are hyperextended. The legs remain straight (knees fully extended).

The swimmer is *arched*.

Axis—An imaginary straight line around which the body rotates in a given position or movement.

1. Longitudinal Axis—The line running through the body from the head to the feet.
2. Lateral Axis—A line running through the body from side to side or from front to back.
3. Horizontal Axis—An axis parallel to the water's surface.
4. Vertical Axis—An axis perpendicular to the water's surface.

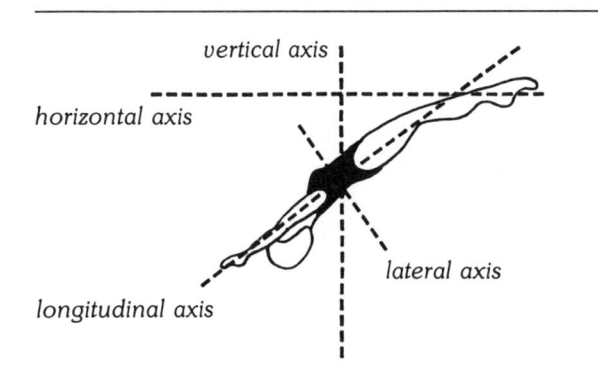

Back or Backward—Toward the back side (spinal side) of the body or moving with the back side leading.

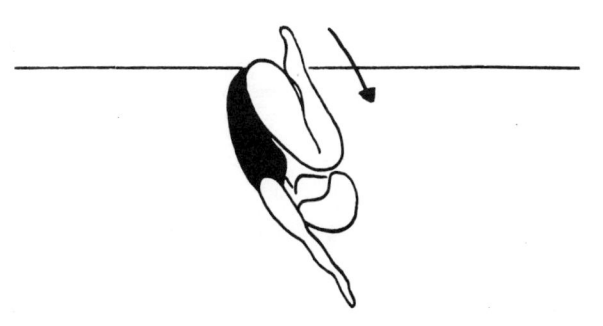

The swimmer is rotating *backward*.

Catch—To feel the pressure of the water with the fingertips and palms.

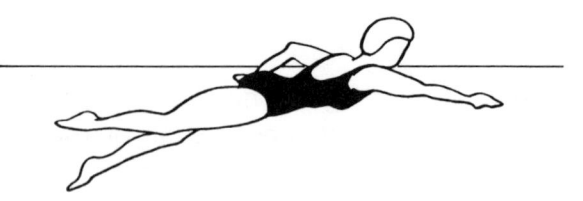

The right arm catches the water.

Compact—Occupying the smallest space possible; body parts are brought as close together as possible.

The swimmer is compact.

Extend—To stretch to the fullest length; to straighten or unbend.

The swimmer is fully extended.

Flex—To bend; to make the angle of a joint as small as possible.

The wrist is flexed.

Front or Forward—Referring to the front side (breast side) of the body, toward the front, or moving with the front side leading.

front side

Hold—To create traction to allow the body to move forward.

The right arm holds the water.

Horizontal—In strict use, parallel to the water surface; sometimes used to indicate nearly, but not exactly, parallel to the surface. The "horizontal" leg would be the leg most closely approximating the horizontal position.

The right leg is horizontal.

Hyperextend—To bend past the normal fully extended position; to bend opposite to the normal direction of bending for a joint.

The wrist is hyperextended.

Perpendicular—Forming a 90-degree angle (right angle).

Parallel—To be the same distance apart at all points. A leg is parallel to the water surface if the upper part of the foot, knee, and thigh are all the same distance from the surface.

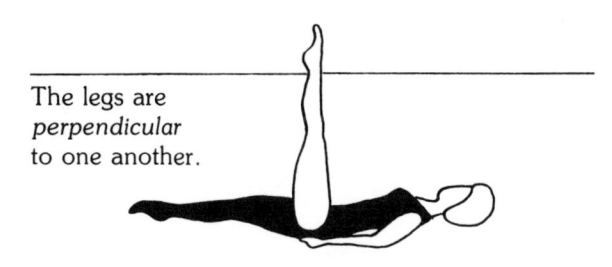

The legs are perpendicular to one another.

The right leg is parallel to the water.

Prone—Lying on the front of the body, or having the front of the body downward.

The swimmer is prone.

Recovery—Returning the arm or leg to the starting position in a nonpropulsive movement.

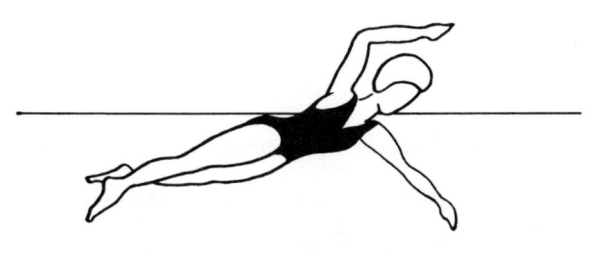

The right arm is in recovery.

Supine — Lying on the back, or having the front of the body upward.

Surface — When used alone, "surface" always refers to the water surface.

Trunk — The body, not including the head or the limbs.

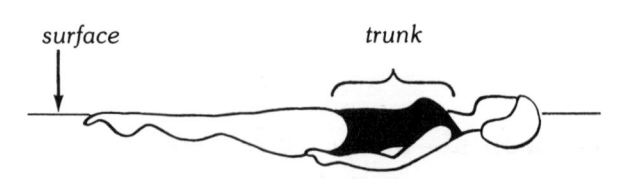

The swimmer is supine.

Vertical — Strictly used, "vertical" means to form a right angle with the water surface, or to be perpendicular to the water surface. "Vertical" is sometimes used to indicate a position which is closer to vertical than to horizontal.

Water Line — The level at which the water surface exists with respect to the body or to parts of the body.

The right leg is vertical.

Basic Body Positions

Body positions make up the foundation of all movements in synchro.

General Position Guidelines — Unless otherwise indicated, the following guidelines apply to all body positions and basic actions:

1. All parts of the body are fully extended.
2. Arm positions are not set; they are open to the needs of the swimmer.

A. Back Layout Position
1. Body in a supine position.
2. Face, hips, thighs, and feet at the surface.

B. Back Pike Position
1. Body bent at hips and as compact as possible.
2. Legs straight and drawn toward chest.

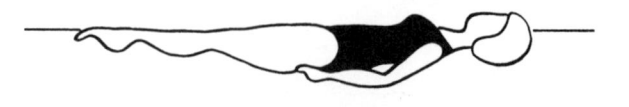

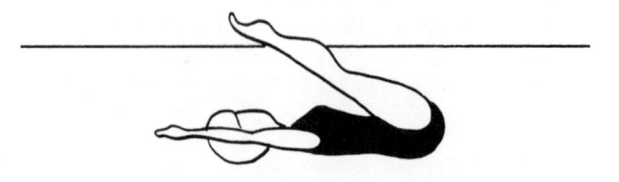

C. Ballet Leg Position

1. Body in back layout position.
2. One leg extended perpendicular to the surface.
3. The face and the foot of the horizontal leg are at the surface.

D. Ballet Leg, Submarine Position

1. Body, head, and one leg extended horizontally, parallel to the surface.
2. One leg extended vertically, perpendicular to the body and the surface.
3. Water line anywhere between the knee and the ankle of the vertical leg.

E. Ballet Leg, Double Position

1. Trunk in supine position.
2. Legs extended and perpendicular to the surface.
3. Trunk and legs form as close to a 90-degree angle as possible.
4. Face at the surface.

F. Ballet Legs, Double, Submarine Position

1. Trunk and head parallel to the surface.
2. Legs extended and perpendicular to both the body and the surface.
3. Water line between the knees and ankles.

G. Bent Knee Position

1. Body in front layout, back layout, vertical, or arched position.
2. One knee bent with the foot of the bent leg on the inside of the opposite leg, at or above the knee. (Exception: In the Bent Knee position used to start or finish a Ballet Leg, the knee is bent just until the thigh of the bent leg is perpendicular to the surface. The foot remains on the inside of the opposite leg.)

Supine

Prone

H. Bent Knee, Double Position

1. Knees drawn toward chest, with feet and head at surface.
2. Thighs perpendicular to surface.

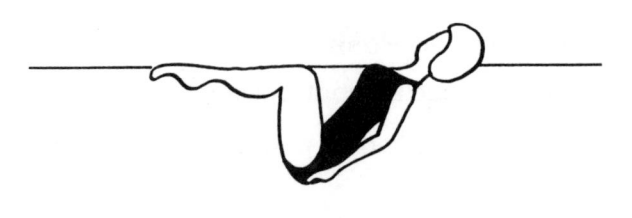

I. Circle Position

1. Head, buttocks, and feet follow the arc of a circle.

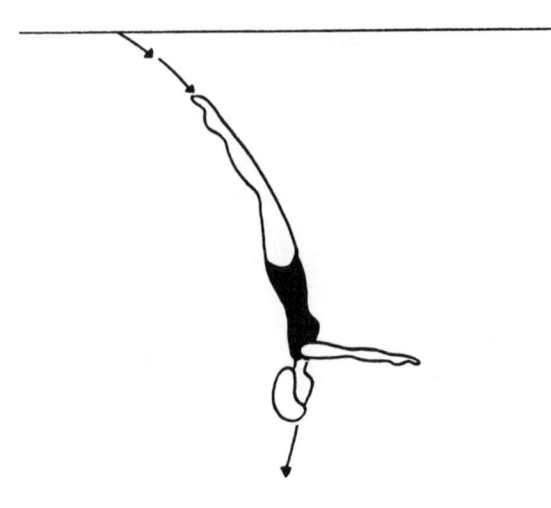

J. Crane Position

1. Body and one leg in vertical position with head down.
2. Head, hip, and ankle of the vertical leg in line with body, and the horizontal leg at a right angle to the trunk and parallel to the surface.
3. Water line anywhere between the hip and ankle.

K. Fishtail Position

1. Body position same as in Crane position, except with the foot of the horizontal leg at the surface regardless of the depth of the hips.

L. Flamingo position

1. One leg extended vertically, perpendicular to the surface.
2. Other leg extended horizontally and drawn toward the chest, with the midcalf opposite the vertical leg and the foot at the surface.

M. Flamingo, Submarine Position

1. Trunk and head extended horizontally, parallel to the surface.
2. One leg extended perpendicular to the body and the surface.
3. Other leg drawn toward the chest, with the mid-calf opposite the vertical leg and the shin parallel to the surface.
4. Water line between knee and ankle of vertical leg.

N. Front Layout Position

1. Body extended in a prone position.
2. Shoulder, buttocks, and heels at the surface.
3. Face in or out of the water.

O. Front Pike Position

1. Body bent at hips to form a 90-degree angle.
2. Legs straight.
3. Head in line with trunk.

P. Front Pike, Surface Position

1. Trunk and head extended perpendicular to the surface, head downward.
2. Heels, thighs, and buttocks at the surface with legs perpendicular to the body.

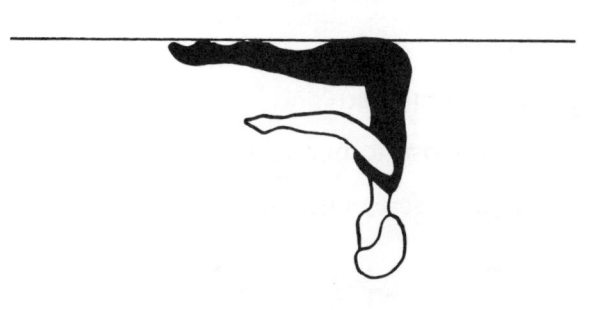

Q. Knight Position

1. Trunk arched and vertical, head downward, one leg perpendicular to the surface.
2. Head and shoulders under hips.
3. Other leg extended backward as horizontal as possible, with foot at surface.

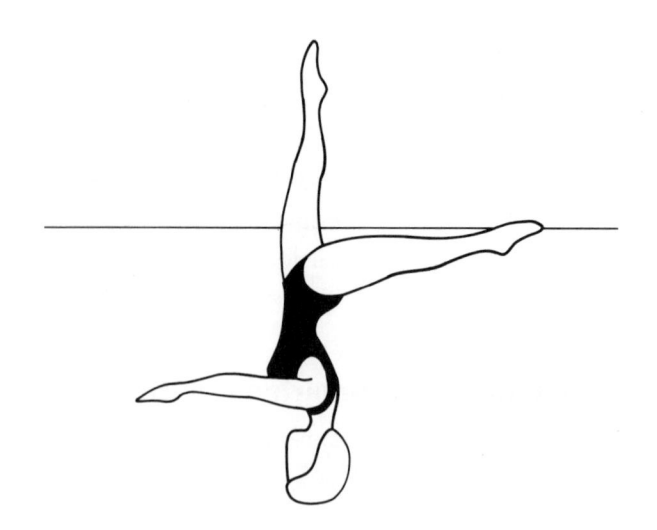

R. Side Layout Position

1. Body extended horizontally on either side.
2. Shoulder, hip, and ankle of top side of body at the surface.
3. Face out of the water.
4. Lower arm extended in line with the body above the head, and upper arm extended in line with the body along the trunk and thigh.

S. Split Position

1. One leg extended forward and other leg extended backward; both feet and hips as near the surface as possible.
2. Trunk arched, shoulders under hips, head vertical.

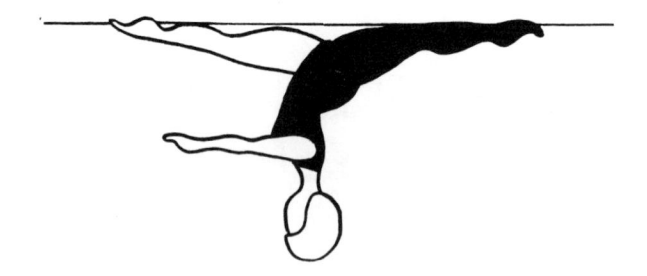

T. Tuck Position

1. Body as compact as possible.
2. Back rounded.
3. Knees together.
4. Heels close to buttocks.
5. Head close to knees.

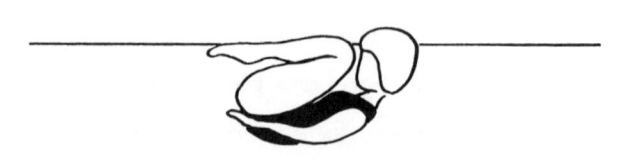

U. Tuck, Vertical Position

1. Body in compact Tuck position.
2. Shoulders and head downward, shins perpendicular to surface.
3. Buttocks just at surface.

V. Vertical Position

1. Body in vertical position, head downward.
2. Head, hips, and ankles in line, and longitudinal line of the body perpendicular to the surface.

And now, on to the skills . . .

UNIT I

Unit I Skill Performance Objectives

Swimmers should be able to perform the following skills for the designated distances or in the designated way.

Strokes and Transitions:

Side Stroke—25 yards

Crawl Stroke—25 yards

Basic Positions and Sculls:

Eel (Standard Scull)—15 yards

Snail (Reverse Standard Scull)—15 yards

Figures:

Tub—Turn to both the left and the right.

Somersault, Back Tuck

Oyster

Water Wheel—Turn to both the left and the right.

Sequence:

Performed to "Syncopated Clock" by Leroy Anderson

Side Stroke

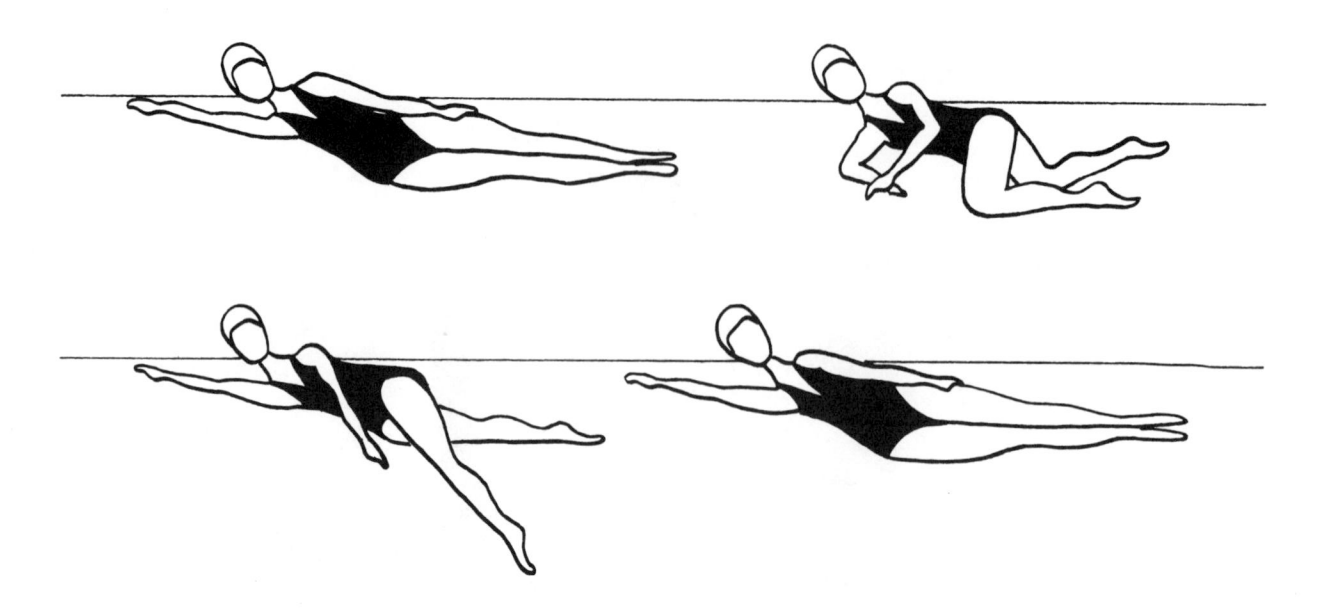

Position for Beginning of Stroke and Glide

The body is in a Side Layout position with the legs fully extended. The lower arm extends above the head in line with the rest of the body and rests on the surface. The chin is in line with the upper shoulder and the face is out of the water. The head should be in line with the rest of the body. The neck shouldn't have to bend forward in order to keep the face out of the water. The top arm is straight and rests on top of the body, with the palm on the thigh.

Key Point: It is important to keep the body fully extended throughout the stroke in order to keep the body high in the water, and to prevent the hips from sagging.

Arm Stroke

The arm stroke consists of five phases—the entry, catch, hold, recovery, and reach.

Entry
The lower, or lead, arm remains fully extended and begins to "pull" on the water, first with the fingertips and then with the palm of the hand.

Catch
The lead elbow flexes, which allows it to slide horizontally over the hand. This movement is performed in line with the body.

Hold
The arm holds the water momentarily and permits the body to move slightly past the arm.

Recovery
While the lower arm holds the water, the elbow of the top arm forms a 90-degree angle and reaches across the chest while staying close to the body. Now the top arm begins to pull on the water as the lower arm goes back to the fully extended position. The hand of the top arm continues to pull as close to the front of the body as possible un-

til the arm straightens again and the palm of the hand is at the thigh.

Reach

At this point, the hand turns slightly at the wrist to enable the palm to "rest" on the thigh. The lower arm is once again fully extended at the surface.

Kick

At the same time at which the arms begin the recovery, both knees are bent simultaneously and the feet are drawn directly towards the buttocks. Once the knees are bent and the feet are close to the buttocks, the top leg is extended in front of the body and the foot is also extended. Simultaneously, the bottom leg straightens in back of the body as far as possible. The legs should reach a Split position. Both legs "catch" and hold the water. Then they come back together, still in a fully extended position.

Kick and Arm Stroke Coordination

The kick recovery begins with the catch portion of the lead arm stroke. The legs remain still in the fully extended position at the end of the kick until the lead arm catch occurs.

Breathing

Swimmers should inhale as their lead arm enters and holds, and exhale during the reach and into the glide portion of the stroke.

Teaching Progression

On the Deck Have the Swimmers:

1. Practice the movement of the lower arm.
2. Practice the movement of the top arm.
3. Practice the entire arm movement.
4. Practice the movement of the top leg.
5. Practice the movement of the top leg and both arms.

Coaching Tip: Have the swimmers work on the strokes while on benches to best simulate their position in the water.

In the Water Have the Swimmers:

1. Perform the entire arm stroke.
2. Perform the kick.
3. Perform the kick and arm stroke together.

Crawl Stroke
(Bent Arm Recovery – Head Up)

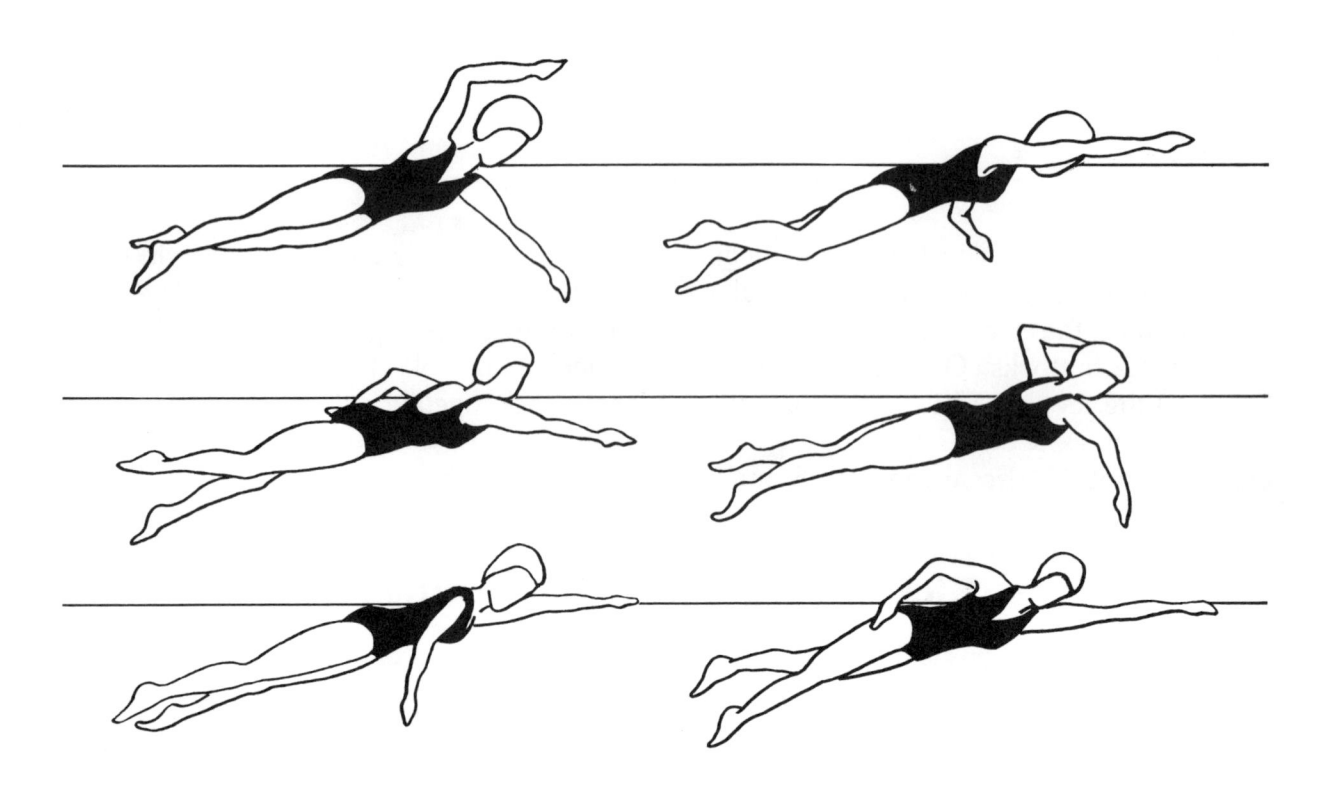

Body Position

The body is in a modified extended prone position. The body is not fully extended because the chin is kept above the water, and the flutter kick is performed deeper in the water than for the standard crawl stroke.

Arm Stroke

The arm stroke for the Crawl consists of the entry, catch, hold, reach, and recovery. The swimmer must have proper shoulder rotation during the stroke to perform correctly.

Entry

The fingers of the lead hand enter the water directly in front of the shoulder and create a "hole" which the arm follows into the water, staying just below the surface. The lead arm continues extending into the hole until the elbow is almost straight.

Catch

As the arm extends into the water, the swimmer begins to feel pressure on the fingertips and palm. When the arm is almost extended, the palm pulls towards the opposite leg.

Hold

The arm holds the water while the body moves forward and over the arm until the hand reaches the leg.

Reach

When the hand reaches the leg, the fingers reach toward the toes and hold the water to provide support for the other arm to make the catch.

Recovery

The recovery begins with the swimmer lifting the shoulder and elbow so that the fingers drag behind the arm. Then the swimmer lifts the elbow over the shoulder, enabling the hand to swing slightly away from the body and forward. While the elbow and shoulder are still high, the hand completes the arc and entry begins again.

During the recovery the palm position is as follows: (a) at the end of the stroke when the hand is by the leg, the palm is up and the fingers point back; (b) when the elbow is at its highest point, the palm is back and the fingers point slightly away from the body and toward the water; (c) during entry the palm is angled down but not flat, and the fingers extend forward.

Shoulder Rotation

Shoulder rotation is critical since the recovery of this stroke is higher than in a standard crawl stroke. At the beginning of the stroke, the shoulder follows the arm into the water. After the arm catches, the shoulder rotates back as the hand reaches for the toes. The swimmer lifts the shoulder again during the recovery. Using proper shoulder rotation will eliminate most sculling movements.

Coordination Check Points

Use the following check points to help coordinate the arm stroke.

1. As one arm makes the catch, the other arm should be extended back at the side of the body with the fingers reaching for the toes.
2. When the pulling arm is at about a right angle to the body, or halfway through the hold, the elbow of the recovery arm should be at its highest point.

Kick

The Flutter kick is a continuous, alternating fluttering movement of the legs. The kick should be shallow enough to provide forward drive for the swimmer without the feet breaking the surface. It must also be deep enough to provide support for the body. Because the head is kept out of the water, the kick needs to be deeper than in the standard Crawl stroke.

Kick and Arm Stroke Coordination

Depending on the speed of the arms and legs, there can be four, six, or eight kicks for every arm stroke. Regardless of the number of kicks per stroke, to maintain proper balance, the downward thrust of one leg should occur as the opposite arm catches. For example, as the left leg thrusts down, the right arm catches.

Breathing

Swimmers should establish a rhythmic breathing pattern. For example, swimmers can inhale on every right arm stroke and exhale slowly the rest of the time.

Teaching Progression

On the Deck Have the Swimmers:

1. Practice one arm at a time.
2. Practice both arms together.

Coaching Tip: Have the swimmers perform the stroke on a bench to best simulate the movement during the stroke.

In the Water Have the Swimmers:

1. Practice the arm strokes in shallow water.
2. Perform the kick with a kickboard and work on adjusting the depth of the kick.
3. Perform the kick without a kickboard while keeping the arms extended forward and the head up.
4. Perform the arm strokes without the kick.
5. Perform the arm strokes with the kick.

Eel (Standard Scull)

The Eel is the standard scull used to support, balance, and/or propel the body forward. When swimmers perform this or any other scull, they must push the water away from the direction in which they want to move. Most of the movement is a pendulum type of action from the elbows to the fingers, with only minimal movement near the shoulders.

The swimmer changes the position of the wrists to obtain the proper direction of movement. To go forward (head-first), as in the Eel, the wrists are hyperextended; to go backward (foot-first), as in the Snail (see p. 24), the wrists are flexed. If the swimmer wants to remain stationary, she extends her hands in line with her forearms and keeps her palms flat, facing the bottom of the pool.

Scull Position and Direction of Movement

- Body extended in a Back Layout position.
- Head and shoulders in line with body.
- Arms at sides of trunk.
- Face, hips, thighs, and feet at the surface.
- Swimmer either remains stationary or moves head-first.

Method of Execution

Once in a proper scull position, the swimmer begins moving by hyperextending her wrists sharply so that the palms turn away from the body. She bends her elbows slightly while keeping her hands close to her body. While keeping her elbows at hip level, the swimmer pushes her palms away from her body, wrists leading, making a sweep of about 12 inches by extending the elbows.

Without stopping, the swimmer rotates her hands so that the palms face the body and the wrists remain hyperextended. Then, by bending her elbows, she sweeps her hands back toward her body with the wrists leading. As soon as the wrists are back at the body, the procedure begins again. The movement of the hands as they go back and forth should resemble a figure eight.

The swimmer must keep the fingers and thumb of the hands close together so that the hands will exert maximum pressure on the water. However, the wrists and elbows must be kept relaxed to maintain a good sweeping motion. Coaching Tip: Have the swimmers imagine that they are smoothing sand.

Teaching Progression

On the Deck Have the Swimmers:

1. Stand with their backs to a wall and their palms flat against the wall. Then have them sharply hyperextend their wrists, lifting their little fingers off the wall while keeping the thumbs pressed against the wall. Next, have the swimmers sweep their hands outward about 12 inches with their thumbs on the wall and the little fingers lifted.

To provide practice in the inward sweeping motion, have the swimmers rotate their hands so that the little fingers are pressing against the wall and the thumbs are lifted. Have them continue the back and forth movement slowly. Emphasize the rotation of the hands at the end of each sweep and the continual wrist hyperextention.

In the Water Have the Swimmers:

1. Stand where the water is shoulder-deep and extend their arms in front of their bodies. On your cue they should (a) rotate their hands outward, (b) sweep them outward, (c) rotate them inward, and (d) sweep them inward. Keep the movement slow.

2. Perform the scull in a Back Layout position with their feet supported by an inner tube or some other flotation device. The swimmers should place all their concentration on their hands. Cue the swimmers with "sweep," "rotate," "sweep," "rotate."

3. Perform the complete scull action, gradually speeding up the movement.

Common Errors

- Rather than an equally strong inward and outward sweep, the inward movement becomes only a resting (recovery) movement. This is finning, not sculling.

- Fingers separate.

Corrections

- Use the cue words "sweep" and "rotate."

- Close fingers.

Common Errors (cont.)

- Stiff, rigid wrists and elbows.
- Movement initiated primarily from the shoulders.
- Feet and hips sinking.

- Failure to maintain wrist hyperextension, especially on inward sweep.
- Failure to extend body fully.

- Failure to extend ankles and toes.
- Allowing hands to break water surface.
- Sculling at waist, thus not supporting the body at its heaviest point.
- Sweeping the hands too far from the body.
- Failure to lead with the wrists.

Corrections (cont.)

- Relax; lead with wrists; "Smooth sand."
- Initiate movement from elbows as much as possible.
- Lift feet to surface. If necessary while learning, drop hips slightly to keep feet at surface. Gradually lift hips.
- Make the hands feel like windshield wipers. Keep palms facing feet.
- Try to be as tall as possible. Stretch. Press head and shoulders back.
- Extend ankles and point toes.
- Scull deeper.
- Scull at hips.

- Don't sweep outward more than about 12 inches.
- Always remember to rotate the wrist and it will be in the correct position to lead.

Snail (Reverse Standard Scull)

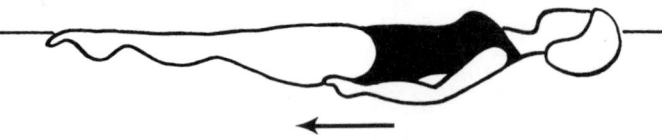

The Snail is executed exactly like the Eel, except that in the Snail the swimmer flexes her wrists in order to move foot-first.

Scull Position and Direction of Movement

- Body extended in a Back Layout position.
- Head and shoulders in line with body.
- Arms at sides of trunk.
- Face, hips, thighs, and feet at the surface.
- Swimmer moves foot-first.

Method of Execution

Once in the scull position, the swimmer moves backward by flexing her wrists sharply and leading with the fingertips instead of the wrists. The remainder of the procedure is exactly the same as in the Eel.

Teaching Progression

Coaches can use the same teaching progression for the Snail as was described for the Eel. Make sure that the swimmers keep their wrists flexed. The procedure for dry land training is outlined below to illustrate the differences.

On the Deck Have the Swimmers:

1. Stand with their arms extended in front of their bodies. Have them begin their practice by sharply flexing their wrists and angling their palms outward, lifting the little finger as much as possible. They should then sweep their hands outward about 12 inches, leading with the fingertips. During the sweep the little fingers should remain lifted and the thumbs should stay down.

To provide practice in the inward sweeping motion, have the swimmers rotate their hands so that the little fingers are down and the thumbs are lifted. Have them continue to perform a slow back and forth movement. Emphasize the rotation of the hands at the end of each sweep and the constant wrist flexion.

Common Errors	Corrections
• Rather than an equally strong inward and outward sweep, the inward movement becomes only a resting (recovery) movement. This is finning, not sculling.	• Use the cue words "sweep" and "rotate."
• Fingers separate.	• Close fingers.
• Stiff, rigid wrists and elbows.	• Relax. It is a little more difficult than in the Eel. Remember to "smooth sand."
• Movement initiated primarily from the shoulders.	• Initiate movement from elbows as much as possible.
• Feet and hips sinking.	• Lift feet to surface. If necessary while learning, drop hips slightly to keep feet at surface. Gradually lift hips.
• Failure to maintain wrist flexion, especially on inward sweep.	• Keep fingertips pointing toward bottom of pool.
• Failure to extend body fully.	• Try to be as tall as possible. Stretch. Press head and shoulders back.
• Failure to extend ankles and toes.	• Extend ankles and point toes.
• Allowing hands to break water surface.	• Scull deeper.

Common Errors (cont.)

- Sculling at waist level, thus, not supporting the body at its heaviest point.
- Sweeping the hands too far from the body.
- Failure to lead with the fingertips.

Corrections (cont.)

- Scull at hips.
- Don't sweep outward more than about 12 inches.
- Always remember to rotate the wrist and the fingertips will be in the correct position to lead.

Tub

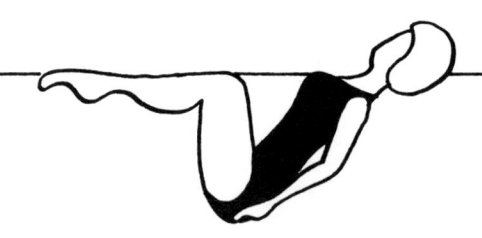

Method of Execution

To perform the Tub figure, the swimmer first assumes a Back Layout position. She initiates the movement into the Tub by slowly drawing her knees toward her chest, keeping both her knees and feet together. As she draws her knees to her chest, her hips will sink. Her head stays in line with her trunk, so her face should be above the water. Her knees, shins, and the tops of her extended feet should remain at the surface throughout the movement. The swimmer continues to draw her knees toward her chest until her thighs are perpendicular to her shins and the water surface. At this point the swimmer is in the Tub position.

From this position the swimmer rotates around an axis which runs perpendicular to the water and through her hips. To turn, the swimmer performs a Snail scull (flexed wrists) with the hand on the side to which she is turning, and an Eel scull (hyperextended wrists) with the other hand. For example, to turn to the right, a swimmer performs a Snail scull with the right hand and an Eel scull with the left. (If the swimmer wants to move either head-first or foot-first in the Tub position, she can perform an Eel scull or Snail scull respectively with both hands. To remain stationary, the swimmer positions her hands so that the palms face the bottom of the pool with flat wrists.)

The swimmer completes the Tub by reversing the procedure she followed to get into the figure. She extends her legs and trunk to return to the Back Layout position.

Teaching Progression

In the Water Have the Swimmers:

1. Get the feel of the position by using the pool gutter to support their feet as they get into a Tub.
2. Work with a partner. The helper supports the swimmer as she executes the figure and watches to make sure the swimmer is performing it correctly.
3. Perform the figure on their own.

Coaching Tip: If the swimmers are having difficulty getting into the Tub position, have them drop their hips deeper.

Common Errors	Corrections
• Lifting head out of the water.	• Press neck and back of head into the water.
• Extraneous movement during the rotation.	• The body should pivot around the hips. Make sure the hands are in the correct position.
• Shins, ankles, and feet sinking under the water.	• Lift feet up and drop hips down.

Somersault, Back Tuck

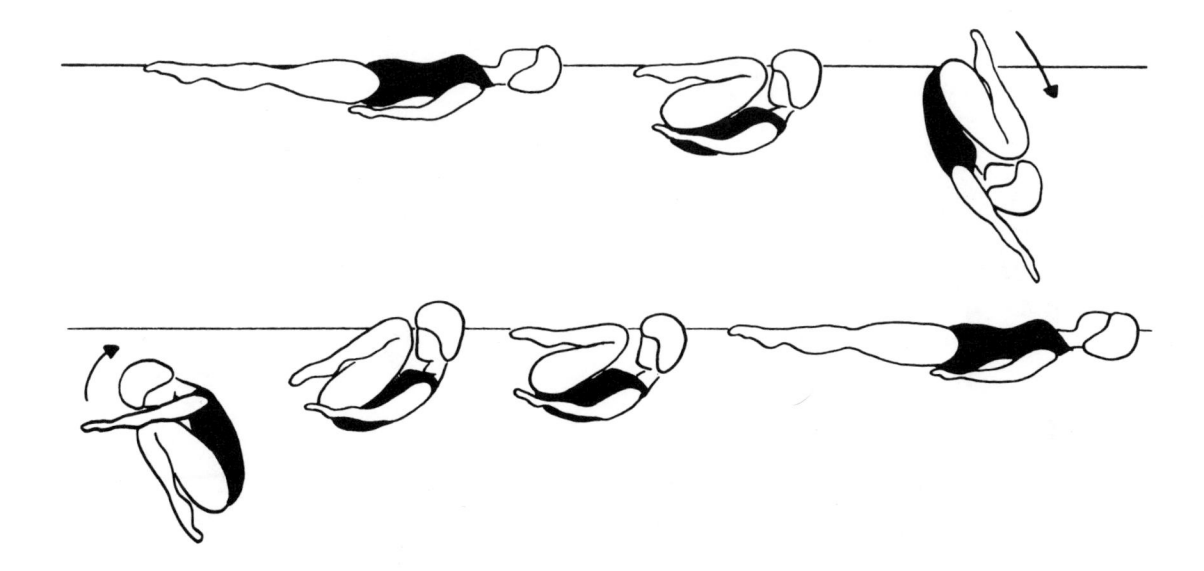

Method of Execution

The swimmer begins the Back Tuck Somersault in a Back Layout position. The swimmer initiates the movement into the figure exactly as if she were performing a Tub; that is, she brings her knees toward her chest as her hips sink. She continues drawing her knees toward her chest, past the Tub position, until her knees are pressed against her chest. At this point the swimmer assumes a full Tuck position (see "Basic Body Positions") by pressing her heels to her buttocks and moving her head forward against her knees.

As soon as she fully assumes the Tuck position, the swimmer begins arm movements which rotate her body backward. The swimmer performs this rotation by moving her hands toward her head, with the palms facing the surface of the water. Then, with straight arms, she pulls toward her hips. This movement rotates the body in the direction opposite the arm movement.

Coaching Tip: Have swimmers imagine turning a jump rope to simulate the arm action.

As swimmers become more advanced, they can learn a more difficult method of rotation. Performing a strong Snail scull with the palms pointed down behind the hips, and lifting the hips while pressing the body backward, will produce body momentum and buoyancy. The momentum and buoyancy will rotate the body until the feet point to the bottom. The swimmer then uses small circular hand movements to return to the basic Tuck position.

The swimmer completes the figure by reversing the procedure and passing through the Tub to return to the Back Layout position.

Teaching Progression

On the Deck Have the Swimmers:

1. Begin to learn the figure by getting into the Tuck position while on a bench. The swimmers can add the arm movements when they are ready.

In the Water Have the Swimmers:

1. Work with a partner. The helper rotates the swimmer once she is in the Tuck position.

2. Perform the movement without a partner.

Common Errors

- Difficulty in rolling backward.

- Throwing the head back to initiate the roll.

- Rolling sideways.

- Sinking too deep on somersault.

- Splashing water.

Corrections

- Tighten the Tuck and check hand position.

- Keep head touching knees.

- Make sure hands exert equal pressure on the water.

- Use smaller arm movements and do not push upward toward surface.

- Keep arm movements small and underwater.

Oyster

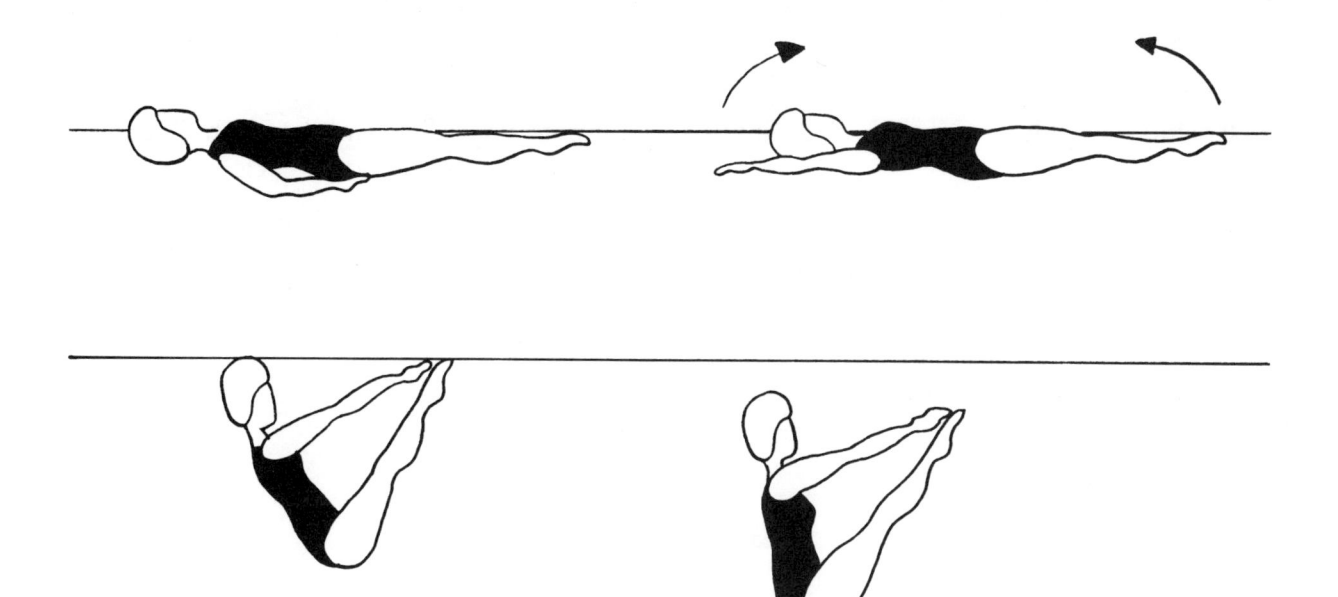

Method of Execution

The swimmer begins the Oyster in a Back Layout position with her hands at her hips. She initiates the movement into the figure by sweeping her arms, with her palms up, away from her body until they are over her head. The arms remain fully extended and under the surface during the movement. Without stopping, she keeps her arms straight and brings them toward the surface, reaching for her feet. Her arms should stay straight and close enough to her head to brush her ears as they come forward.

At the same time, she bends sharply at the hips so that her feet are brought toward her hands as well. As her hands touch the tops of her feet, the body descends in the piked position, hips first. The figure is completed when the feet are submerged. The back remains flat and the head stays in line with the trunk throughout the movement.

Teaching Progression

On the Deck Have the Swimmers:

1. Practice the entire figure.

In the Water Have the Swimmers:

1. Rest their heels on the pool gutter while practicing the arm movement.

2. Perform the entire movement away from the side of the pool.

Common Errors

- Failure to coordinate the hip bend with the arm movement.
- Rolling shoulders forward and lifting head.
- Failure to fully extend ankles and toes.
- Failure to make the arms move continuously from their position at the hips until they touch the feet.

Corrections

- Don't initiate the hip bend until the arms start to move up from the overhead position.
- Keep back flat and head in line with trunk. Press shoulders back.
- Extend ankles and point toes.
- Don't stop the movement at any point.

Water Wheel

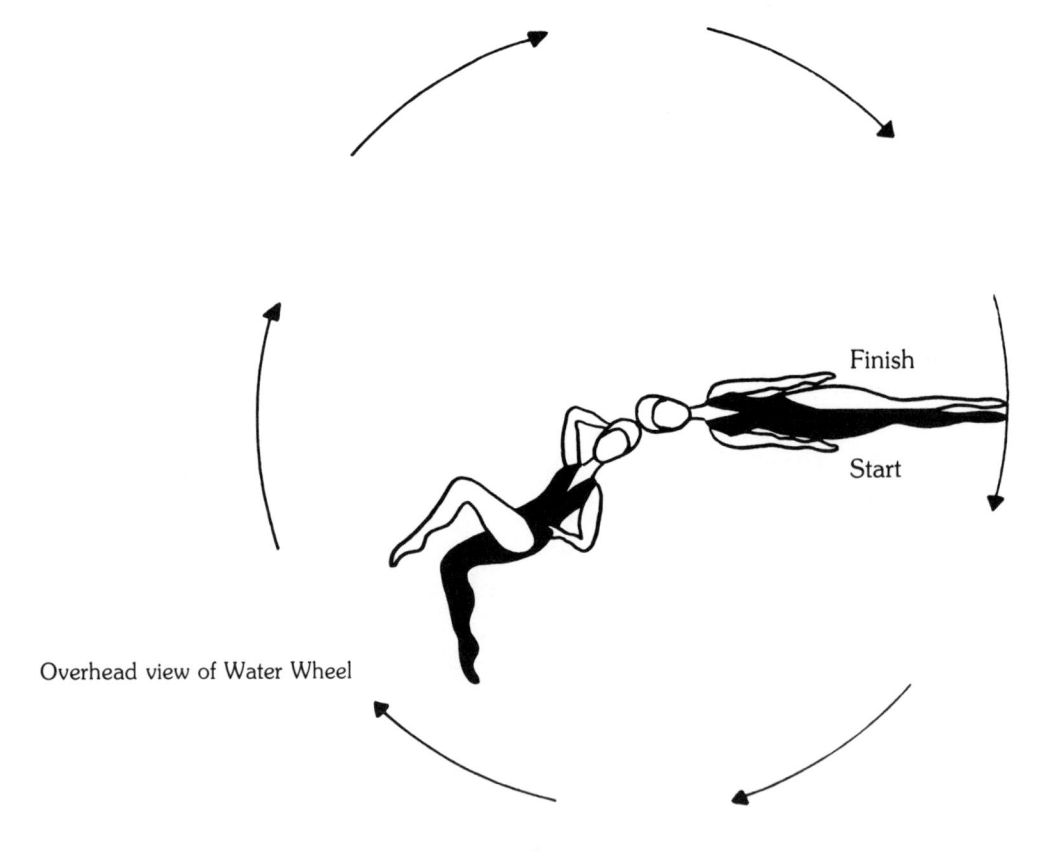

Overhead view of Water Wheel

Method of Execution

The swimmer begins the Water Wheel in a Back Layout position. She initiates the movement into the figure by rotating her hips to the side so that one hip points up and the other down. At the same time, she keeps her shoulders flat and her head in line with her shoulders. Her feet, legs, and hips all should stay close to the surface.

The swimmer rotates around an axis which is in front of her stomach and perpendicular to the surface. This rotation is created by the pedaling action of the legs and feet, which perform a movement similar to pedaling a bicycle. The swimmer should extend her ankles as her feet push away from her body, and flex them as they come toward her body. After the swimmer completes one full revolution, she rotates her hips back and extends her legs into a Back Layout position.

The position of the swimmer's arms during the figure is open to the swimmer. However, she must not scull with them. The body must be propelled only by the legs and feet. The swimmer may want to put her hands on her hips, or put one hand on her hip and the other at the back of her neck.

Teaching Progression

On the Deck Have the Swimmers:

1. Get a feel for the proper position by rotating the hips while keeping the shoulders flat.

In the Water Have the Swimmers:

1. Start in a Back Layout position and rotate their hips to one side. They should concentrate on keeping their legs at the surface. From this position, have them bend their knees and place the foot of one leg on the knee of the other. Keeping their legs in this position, they should use their arms to scull in a circle around the proper axis.

2. Practice the figure using the pedaling action of their feet and legs, along with a scull.

3. Practice the figure without sculling.

Common Errors	Corrections
• Turning the whole body on its side.	• Rotate the hips and legs only.
• Head goes forward with the chin tucked, and the ears come out of the water.	• Press the head and shoulders back.
• Hips, legs, and feet drop below the surface.	• Lift legs and feet, and press head and shoulders back.
• Body not rotating on the proper axis.	• Bend knees sharply during the pedaling action.

SEQUENCE 1

"Syncopated Clock" by Leroy Anderson

The first sequence uses all of the skills learned in Unit I. The precise movements the swimmers need to perform during the beats are listed on the chart below. Teach each line by itself, adding the next line when the swimmers are ready. Once the swimmers learn all four lines of a section, have them perform the whole section several times. Then attack the next section (once again, line by line) until they memorize all four lines. Have them perform this section several times. Now put the two sections together. Once the swimmers can perform the first two sections together, proceed to the third section. Continue this process until the swimmers learn the whole sequence.

Coaching Tip: Swimmers will enjoy, and often benefit from, seeing the entire sequence performed before they start to learn it. Seeing the sequence helps give the swimmers a mental image of what they are trying to create.

The movements choreographed on the chart take the swimmers through the first 16 measures of the music. They can continue to repeat these movements for the rest of the song.

During the sequence, swimmers will move approximately 20 yards in a straight line. If they continue along with the music, they can reverse direction or continue in the same direction, remembering to turn when they reach the side of the pool.

SEQUENCE 1
Music: "Syncopated Clock" by Leroy Anderson

Measures	Beats: 1	2	3	4
Introduction	X X	X X	X X	X X
1	Right side scissors kick	Left arm Crawl	Left side scissors kick	Right arm Crawl
2	Right side scissors kick	Left arm Crawl	Left side scissors kick	Right arm Crawl
3	Right Side Stroke	Glide	Right Side Stroke	Roll on to back on right arm
4	Eel scull, traveling	⎯⎯⎯⎯⎯⎯⎯⎯⎯⎯⟶		Eel scull, stationary

Sequence 1 (cont.)

	Water Wheel to right:			
5	Turn hips to side	Right leg pedal	Left leg pedal	Right leg pedal
6	Left leg pedal	Right leg pedal	Left leg pedal	Right leg pedal
7	Extend left leg	Extend right leg	Back Layout	Hold in Back Layout
8	Snail scull, traveling	⎯⎯⎯⎯⎯⎯⎯⎯⟶		Tub position

	Tub to right:			
9	Turn to 1/8	Turn to 1/4	Turn to 3/8	Turn to 1/2
10	Turn to 5/8	Turn to 3/4	Turn to 7/8	Complete full turn
11	Extend legs to Back Layout	Stretch body	Hold in Back Layout	
12	Oyster	⎯⎯⎯⎯⎯⎯⎯⎯⟶		Return to surface

13	Right side scissors kick	Left arm Crawl	Left side scissors kick	Right arm Crawl
14	Right side scissors kick	Left arm Crawl	Left side scissors kick	Roll to back on left arm
	Somersault, Back Tuck:			
15	Tuck	Roll	Roll	Return to surface
16	Extend legs	Stretch	Turn over onto stomach, tuck knees under hips to a vertical position	Head up, smile!

UNIT II

Unit II Skill Performance Objectives

Swimmers should be able to perform the following skills for the designated distances or in the designated way.

Strokes and Transitions:

Back Stroke—25 yards

Breast Stroke—25 yards

Basic Positions and Sculls:

Canoe Scull—15 yards

Alligator Scull—15 yards

Torpedo Scull—15 yards

Figures:

Corkscrew—One each direction

Log Roll—One each direction

Somersault, Front Pike

Jumpover

Sequence:

Performed to "California Girls" by the Beach Boys

Back Stroke

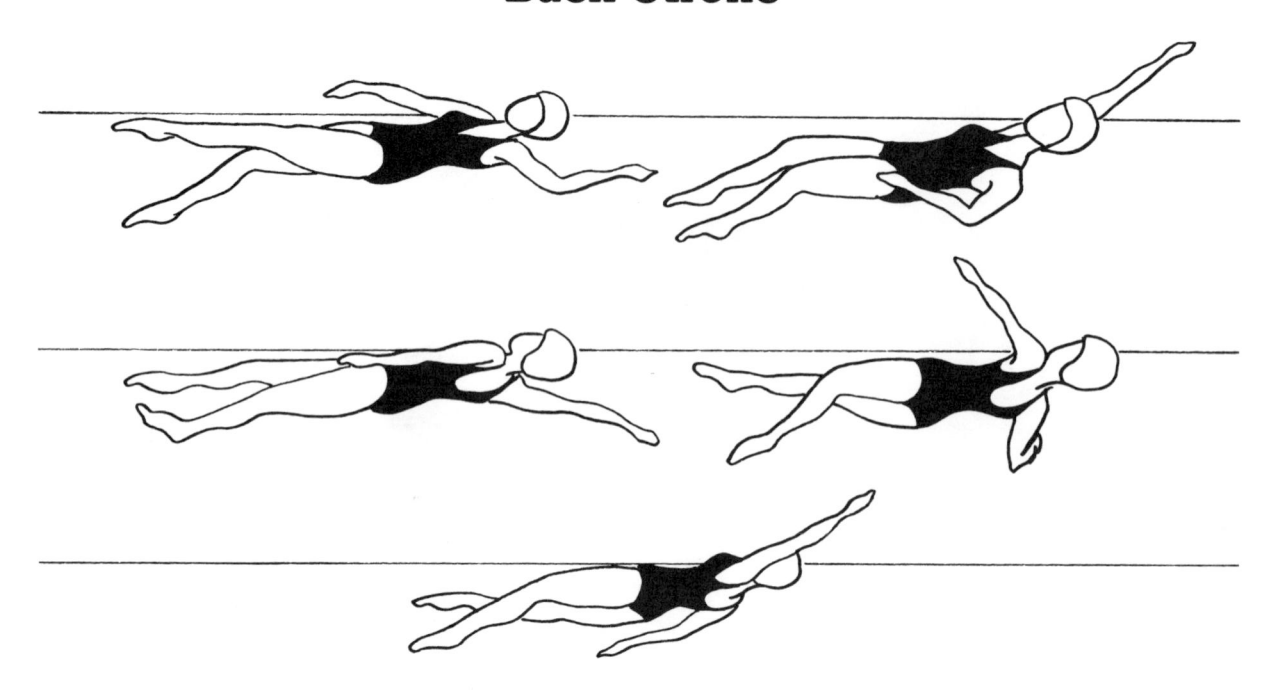

Body Position

The body is in a slightly modified Back Layout position. The head should be held slightly higher than in the standard back stroke, which will lower the hips slightly in the water. This permits the swimmer to kick without breaking the surface.

Arm Stroke

The arms should be fully extended during the recovery phase of the stroke. Shoulder rotation is necessary to allow the arm to extend completely. During the arm stroke, the arms work sequentially as in the Crawl, rather than together. They are always performing opposite parts of the stroke. To visualize the position of the arms in relation to one another, think of them as hands on a clock that are always thirty minutes apart.

Entry

The palm faces outward and the little finger enters the water first, directly in line with the shoulder. As in the Crawl, the rest of the hand, the arm, and the shoulder follow the little finger into the same "hole."

Catch

As the arm drives into the water, the swimmer begins to push with her hand. Initially, the palm faces down and then slightly away from the body. As the hand continues to push, the elbow flexes until it forms a right angle. At this point the fingers are pointing toward the water surface and the elbow is directly below the shoulder.

Hold

When the elbow is at a right angle, the arm holds the water and allows the body to move past the hand and arm. The shoulder rotates beneath the water toward the toes to permit the arm to hold.

Reach

The swimmer continues the stroke by flexing her wrist and reaching for her toes. The hand holds again when the thumb and knuckles are just below the bathing suit line to provide support until the other arm makes the catch. After the other arm makes the catch, the reaching arm extends fully to prepare for the recovery.

Recovery

The recovery begins with the swimmer lifting the shoulder and "sneaking" the little-finger side of the hand out of the water with minimal water movement by the arm. The arm stays fully extended and forms a high arc passing over the shoulder. The shoulder should remain above the surface throughout the recovery and until it follows the arm into the water again in the entry phase.

Coaching Tip: Have the swimmers simulate the arm movement out of the water by imagining a string attached to the little-finger side of their hand which is being pulled from above.

Palm Position During the Stroke

Right before the recovery, the palm is down while the fingers reach for the toes. At the high point of recovery, when the arm is extended vertically over the shoulder, the thumb is turned toward the body and the little finger is turned away from the body, so that the palm is facing out and in line with the arm. As the arm descends, the hand rotates so that the little finger is closest to the water and the palm faces down slightly toward the water.

Shoulders

It is crucial that the shoulder rotation be complete in order for the stroke to be strong and appear effortless. After the shoulder follows the arm into the water, it drops or rolls below the plane of the body to be in position for a good catch. The shoulder must continue to rotate toward the toes as the body passes over the arm in the hold phase. During the recovery, the shoulder leaves the water, followed by the upper arm, forearm, and finally the hand. If the shoulder doesn't rotate properly, there will be unnecessary stress placed on the arm through the catch, hold, and recovery phases.

Kick

The Back Flutter kick is similar to the Flutter kick used in the Crawl. It is a continuous, alternating fluttering motion of the legs. The toes should be turned in slightly during the kick. When the leg is going up, the swimmer will feel the water pressure on the wide part of the front of the foot. On the downward movement, the swimmer will feel the pressure on the heel and the bottom of the big toe. Equal pressure must be used during the up and down movement of the kick in order to achieve proper body balance.

Kick and Arm Stroke Coordination

Depending on the speed of the arms and legs, there can be four, six, or eight kicks for every arm stroke. Regardless of the number of kicks per stroke, to maintain proper balance, the upward thrust of one leg should occur as the opposite arm catches. For example, as the left leg thrusts up, the right arm catches.

Breathing

Swimmers should breath in a rhythmic pattern, inhaling during the recovery phase of one arm and exhaling during the recovery phase of the other.

Teaching Progression

On the Deck Have the Swimmers:

1. Practice one arm at a time while standing on the deck or lying on a bench.
2. Practice both arms together while standing on the deck or lying on a bench.

In the Water Have the Swimmers:

1. Practice the arm strokes without kicking.
2. Practice the kick without a kickboard by keeping the hands extended overhead in line with the body.
3. While using the kick, practice the arm stroke with the right arm only and then with the left arm only.
4. While using the kick, practice the arm stroke using only one arm at a time, keeping the other arm overhead until the opposite arm finishes the entire stroke cycle.
5. Combine the arm stroke and the kick.

Breast Stroke
(Head Up)

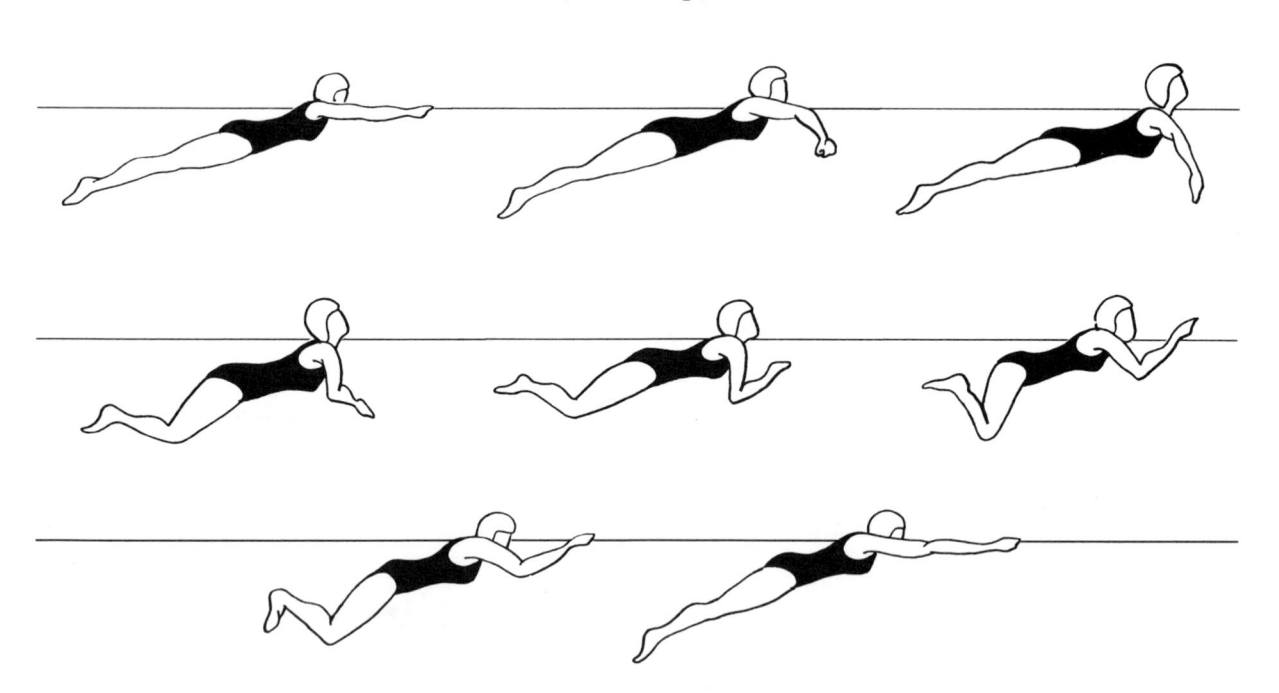

Starting and Glide Position

The body is in a modified extended Front Layout position. The head stays above the water, with the chin just above the surface. The arms start fully extended in a horizontal plane with the shoulders. The backs of the thumbs almost touch and the palms face slightly outward. The legs are also fully extended but on a plane just lower than the body.

Arm Stroke

The arm stroke consists of five phases—the entry, catch, hold, scull, and recovery.

Entry

From the starting position, both arms press out, back, and slightly down toward the body. They move to a position that is halfway between where the hands started and where they would be if they were held out to the sides of the body. The elbows begin to flex as they near this halfway position.

Catch

The elbows continue to flex until the fingertips point toward the bottom of the pool and the arms form a 90-degree angle. Because of the position of the body, there is considerably more elbow action in the catch phase of the modified stroke than in the standard stroke.

Hold

The arms hold the water as the body moves forward and the shoulders pass through the arms.

Scull (also called the "Power Phase")

At this point, the forearms and hands slide inward and forward. The elbows should meet below the rib cage at the same time that the thumbs meet under the chin. This movement keeps the swimmer high in the water during the recovery phase of the kick. This action is different from the similar phase of the standard stroke because there is more elbow action.

Recovery

As the arms continue to slide forward, the swimmer should rotate them slightly so that the backs of the elbows are higher than the insides of the elbows and the thumbs are lower than the little fingers. The recovery is finished with the arms once again fully extended and in line with the shoulders.

Shoulder Rotation

The swimmer must have complete shoulder rotation for the stroke to be strong and appear effortless.

Kick

From the starting position, the hips and knees flex, drawing the heels straight towards the buttocks, with the ankles and toes flexed. When the heels are on a plane closer to the buttocks than the knees, the swimmer should begin to push the feet just outside of the hips, back, and slightly downward until her knees straighten. Without pausing, she should straighten her ankles and point her toes. She "holds" or continues to push the water with her calves and big toes until the arm entry phase begins and the knees come together.

Kick and Arm Stroke Coordination

The leg action begins toward the end of the entry phase. The pushing action of the feet will propel the body forward while the arms move forward in the scull and recovery phases. The legs hold until the arms are back into the fully extended position, and they complete their movement as the arms begin the entry phase.

Coaching Tip: Tell the swimmers to "kick" their arms into the recovery.

Breathing

Swimmers should maintain a rhythmic breathing pattern by inhaling during the hold and scull phases and exhaling during the recovery.

Teaching Progression

On the Deck Have the Swimmers:

1. Practice the arm stroke while either standing on the deck or lying on a bench.
2. Practice the leg kick on the end of a bench or on the diving board.

In the Water Have the Swimmers:

1. Bend at the waist while standing in shallow water and practice the arm stroke.
2. Practice the leg kick with a kickboard.
3. Combine the arm stroke with the kick.

Canoe Scull

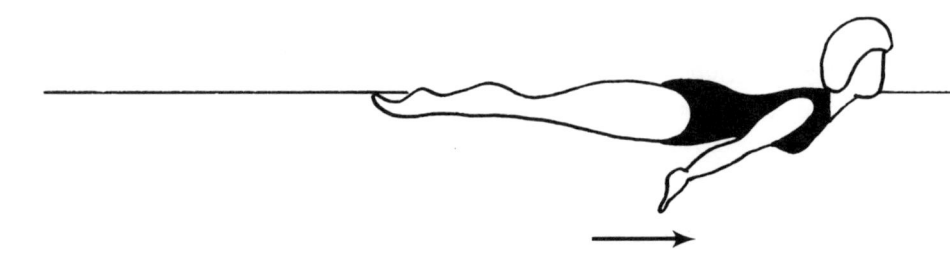

Scull Position and Direction of Movement

- Body extended in Front Layout position.
- Lower back arched slightly to keep the head, buttocks, and heels at the surface.
- Swimmer either remains stationary or moves head-first.

During the Canoe scull the body moves head-first or remains stationary. The position of the face and arms is optional. The face can be in or out of the water, and the arms can be anywhere between the hips and shoulders. The body build and buoyancy of the swimmer will dictate the most effective position for the arms.

Method of Execution

The swimmer gets into a Front Layout position and places her arms in the same plane as her body in a comfortable position between her hips and shoulders. She hyperextends her wrists sharply and turns her palms outward, facing away from her body. Her elbows are bent and her hands are almost touching underneath her body.

Just as in the Eel, the swimmer leads with her wrists and sweeps her hands out from her body about 12 inches by extending her elbows. Without pausing, she then rotates her hands so that the palms face inward and sweeps her hands back toward each other by bending the elbows. The movement of the hands as they go back and forth should resemble a figure eight. The swimmer must keep her fingers and thumb close together in order to exert maximum pressure on the water, but keep the wrists and elbows relaxed to ensure a smooth sweeping motion.

Coaching Tip: Have swimmers imagine they are smoothing sand to develop the proper hand motion.

The swimmer maintains the arched position by pressing up with her heels and slightly down with her shoulders. This will keep her horizontal in the water.

Movement

If the swimmer wants to remain stationary, she keeps her palms facing the bottom of the pool. If she wants to travel forward, her fingertips should face the bottom of the pool.

Teaching Progression

On the Deck Have the Swimmers:

1. Stand and extend their forearms out in front of their body by bending their arms and keeping the elbows close to the body. Have them hyperextend their wrists so that their palms face away from their body. With the wrists hyperextended, they should then turn their palms out so that the little fingers are lifted and the thumbs are pressed down. From this position, the swimmers should sweep their hands out about 12 inches by extending the elbows and leading with the wrists. At the end of the sweep, the swimmers should rotate their hands so that the palms face inward, with the thumbs lifted and the little fingers pressed down. Then they should sweep their hands back by bending the elbows, still with the wrists leading. Have the swimmers continue the movement slowly. Emphasize the hand rotation at the end of each sweep and the constant wrist hyperextension.

In the Water Have the Swimmers:

1. Practice the movement in a Front Layout position with their feet hooked over the pool gutter. Use the cues "rotate out," "sweep out," "rotate in," and "sweep in."
2. Practice in the Front Layout position with their feet in an inner tube or some other flotation device. Continue to use cues.
3. Practice in the proper position, with the cues "sweep" and "rotate."
4. Speed up the motion as they learn it.

Common Errors

- Rather than an equally strong inward and outward sweep, the inward movement becomes only a resting (recovery) movement. This is finning, not sculling.

Corrections

- Use the cue words "sweep" and "rotate."

Common Errors (cont.)	Corrections (cont.)
• Fingers separate.	• Close fingers.
• Stiff, rigid wrists and elbows.	• Relax; lead with wrists; "Smooth sand."
• Movement initiated primarily from the shoulders.	• Initiate movement from elbows as much as possible.
• Feet and hips sinking.	• Learning the scull with the face in the water will make it easier to lift the feet and hips. Make sure to press the heels up onto the surface.
• Failure to maintain wrist hyperextention, especially on the inward sweep.	• Make the forearms and hands feel like windshield wipers.
• Failure to extend ankles and toes.	• Extend ankles and point toes.
• Sweeping the hands too far from the body.	• Don't sweep outward more than about 12 inches.
• Failure to lead with the wrist.	• Always remember to rotate the wrist and it will be in the correct position to lead.

Alligator Scull

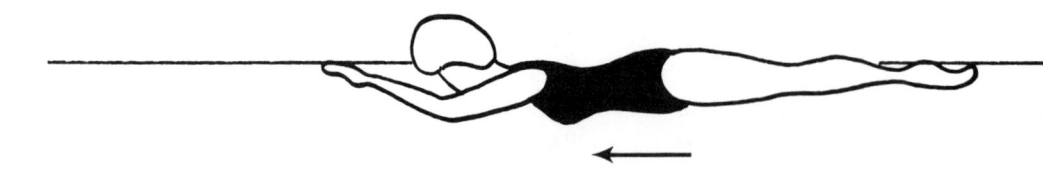

Scull Position and Direction of Movement

- Body extended in Front Layout position.
- Lower back arched slightly to keep the head, buttocks, and heels at the surface.
- Face in the water so that the eyes can watch for proper hand movement.
- Arms extended forward at about a 30- to 45-degree angle toward the side or bottom of the pool, depending on the body build and buoyancy of the swimmer.
- Swimmer either remains stationary or moves head-first.

Method of Execution

The swimmer gets into a Front Layout position with her arms overhead and slightly bent at the elbows. She flexes her wrists sharply and turns her palms outward, facing away from her body.

Just as in the Snail, the swimmer leads with her fingertips, pressing her palms out away from the body in a 12-inch sweep by extending her elbows. Without pausing, she then rotates her hands so that the palms face the body and sweeps the hands back toward each other by bending the elbows. The fingertips continue to lead the movement, and the wrists remain flexed. The movement of the hands as they go back and forth should resemble a figure eight. The swimmer must keep her fingers and thumb close together in order to exert maximum pressure on the water, but keep the wrists and elbows relaxed to ensure a smooth sweeping motion.

Coaching Tip: Have the swimmers imagine they are smoothing sand to develop the proper hand motion.

The swimmer maintains the arched position by pressing up with her heels and slightly down with her shoulders. This will keep her horizontal in the water.

Teaching Progression

On the Deck Have the Swimmers:

1. Stand and extend their forearms out in front of their body by bending their arms. Direct them to flex their wrists sharply and angle their palms out. They should then lift their little fingers and press the thumbs down as they sweep their hands outward about 12 inches by extending their elbows and leading with the fingertips. At the end of the sweep, the swimmers are to rotate their hands so that the palms face the body, with the thumbs lifted and the little fingers pressed down. Then the hands are swept back inward by bending the elbows, still with the wrists leading. Have the swimmers continue the movement slowly. Emphasize the hand rotation at the end of each sweep and the constant wrist flexion.

In the Water Have the Swimmers:

1. Stand where it is shoulder-deep and extend their arms in front of their bodies at an angle of 30- to 45-degrees. Have them perform the sculling action slowly while you give the cues of "rotate outward, sweep outward," and "rotate inward, sweep inward." Emphasize wrist flexion throughout.
2. Practice the movement in a Front Layout position with their feet in an inner tube or other flotation devise. Use the cues "rotate out," "sweep out," "rotate in," and "sweep in." Swimmers should be concentrating totally on the movement of their hands.
3. Practice in the proper position, with the cues "sweep" and "rotate."
4. Speed up the motion as they learn it.

Common Errors

- Rather than an equally strong inward and outward sweep, the inward movement becomes only a resting (recovery) movement. This is finning, not sculling.

Corrections

- Use the cue words "sweep" and "rotate."

Common Errors (cont.)	Corrections (cont.)
• Fingers separate.	• Close fingers.
• Stiff, rigid wrists and elbows.	• Relax; lead with fingertips; "Smooth sand."
• Movement initiated primarily from the shoulders.	• Initiate movement from elbows as much as possible.
• Feet and hips sinking.	• Lift the heels to the surface. Support the feet on an inner tube to keep the feet at the surface while learning.
• Failure to maintain wrist flexion, especially on the inward sweep.	• Keep the fingertips pointing toward the bottom of the pool.
• Failure to extend ankles and toes.	• Extend ankles and point toes.
• Sweeping the hands too far from the body.	• Don't sweep outward more than about 12 inches.
• Failure to lead with the fingertips.	• Always remember to rotate the wrist and the fingertips will be in the correct position to lead.

Torpedo Scull

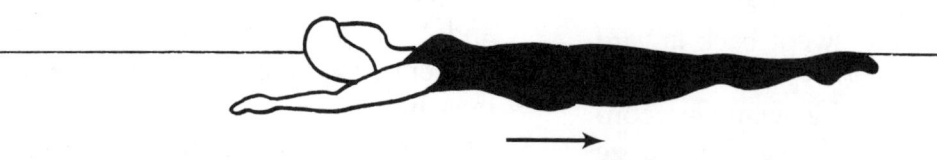

Scull Position and Direction of Movement

- Body in a Back Layout position.
- Arms extended overhead.
- Head and shoulders in line with body.
- Face, hips, thighs, and feet at the surface.
- Swimmer moves foot-first.

Method of Execution

From a Back Layout position, the swimmer gently slides her arms up the sides of her body to a position overhead. She hyperextends her wrists sharply and turns her palms outward, facing away from her body. She bends her elbows slightly which makes her hands almost touch.

Just as in the Eel, the swimmer leads with her wrists and sweeps her hands out from her body about 12 inches by extending her elbows. Without pausing, she then rotates her hands so that the palms face inward and sweeps her hands back toward each other by bending the elbows. At the end of this sweep, the hands will almost touch again. The movement of the hands as they go back and forth should resemble a figure eight. The swimmer must keep her fingers and thumb close together in order to exert maximum pressure on the water, but keep the wrists and elbows relaxed to ensure a smooth sweeping motion.

Coaching Tip: Have swimmers imagine they are smoothing sand to develop the proper hand motion.

Teaching Progression

On the Deck Have the Swimmers:

1. Stand with their arms extended overhead. Direct them to hyperextend their wrists sharply, turning their palms out so that the little fingers press down and the thumbs are lifted. From this position, they are to sweep their hands out about 12 inches by extending the elbows and leading with the wrists. At the end of the sweep, the swimmers should rotate their hands so that the palms face each other, and press down with their thumbs while lifting the little fingers. Then have them sweep their hands back by bending the elbows, still with the wrists leading. Have the swimmers continue the movement slowly. Emphasize the hand rotation at the end of each sweep and the constant wrist hyperextension.

In the Water Have the Swimmers:

1. Practice the sculling movement while their torsos are supported by a partner. Use the cues "rotate out," "sweep out," "rotate in," and "sweep in."

2. Practice in the Back Layout position with their feet supported by an inner tube or some other flotation device. Continue to use cues. Swimmers should be concentrating totally on their hand movements.

3. Practice in the proper position, with the cues "sweep" and "rotate."

4. Start with their hands at their sides and initiate the foot-first movement by sweeping the arms to the overhead position. As soon as the hands are overhead, they should start the sculling motion. Starting the foot-first movement before the hand motion will help prevent the feet from sinking.

5. Take a deep breath and start the Torpedo scull with the body under the water. As their bodies surface, the swimmers should raise their chests and tighten their stomach muscles to stay on top of the water.

6. Speed up the motion as they learn it.

Common Errors	**Corrections**
• Rather than an equally strong inward and outward sweep, the inward movement becomes only a resting (recovery) movement. This is finning, not sculling.	• Use the cue words "sweep" and "rotate."
• Fingers separate.	• Close fingers.
• Stiff, rigid wrists and elbows.	• Relax; lead with wrists; "Smooth sand."
• Movement initiated primarily from the shoulders.	• Initiate movement from the elbows as much as possible.
• Feet and hips sinking.	• Lift feet to surface. Tighten stomach muscles and loosen buttock muscles. Learn the scull with the body submerged.
• Failure to maintain wrist hyperextension, especially on inward sweep.	• Make the forearms and hands feel like windshield wipers. Keep the palms facing away from the body.
• Failure to extend ankles and toes.	• Extend ankles and point toes.
• Hands break the surface.	• Scull deeper.
• Sweeping the hands too far from the body.	• Don't sweep outward more than about 12 inches.
• Lifting the head.	• Press head and shoulders back in line with the body.
• Failure to lead with the wrists.	• Always remember to rotate the wrist and it will be in the correct position to lead.

Corkscrew

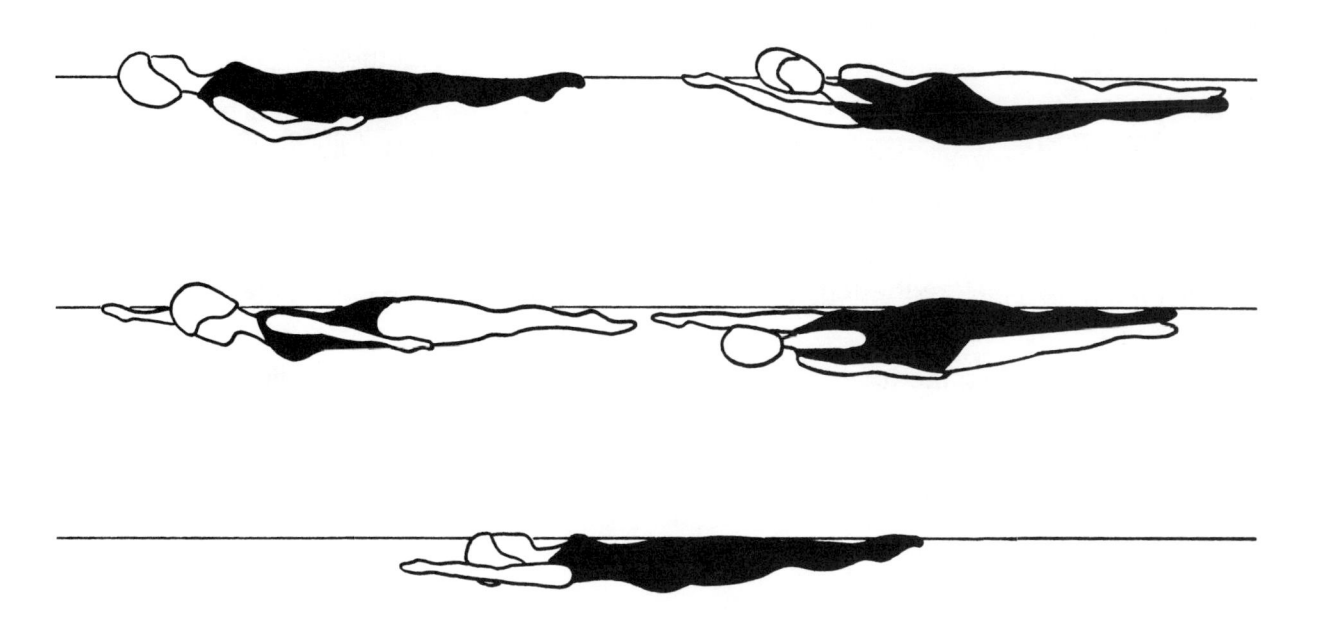

Method of Execution

To perform the Corkscrew the swimmer first assumes a Back Layout position. She begins the figure by simultaneously rotating her body to one side and extending the bottom arm over her head. This is the same Side Layout position that is used in the Side Stroke (see p. 18). The swimmer continues the figure by pressing her head against the extended arm while rolling onto her face. She then lifts the side of her body on which the arm is extended and presses down with the other side of her body. The movement continues until the swimmer has made one complete horizontal revolution and returns to the Back Layout position. The swimmer must keep all her muscles tight in order to make her body roll as a unit in the fully extended position.

Teaching Progression

On the Deck Have the Swimmers:

1. Practice the Back, Front, and Side Layout positions.
2. Perform the entire Corkscrew while standing, so that they can get the feel of the movement.

In the Water Have the Swimmers:

1. Practice the Back, Front, and Side Layout positions.
2. Execute a Side Stroke followed by a Corkscrew. The momentum created by the stroke makes the figure easier to perform and will give the swimmer a feel for the movement in the water.
3. Practice the Corkscrew from a stationary position.

Common Errors	**Corrections**
• Kicking.	• There must be no kicking. Squeeze the legs tightly together.
• Body arched.	• Do not press the shoulders back. Tighten the abdomen and lift the chest.
• Folding one leg over the other during the roll.	• Squeeze legs tightly together.
• Shoulder rolling before the hip.	• Tighten muscles and rotate the body as a unit.
• Body turning before the head.	• Focus the eyes in the direction in which the body is turning.
• Rolling halfway and not being able to continue.	• Lift one side of the body and press down with the other side.

Log Roll

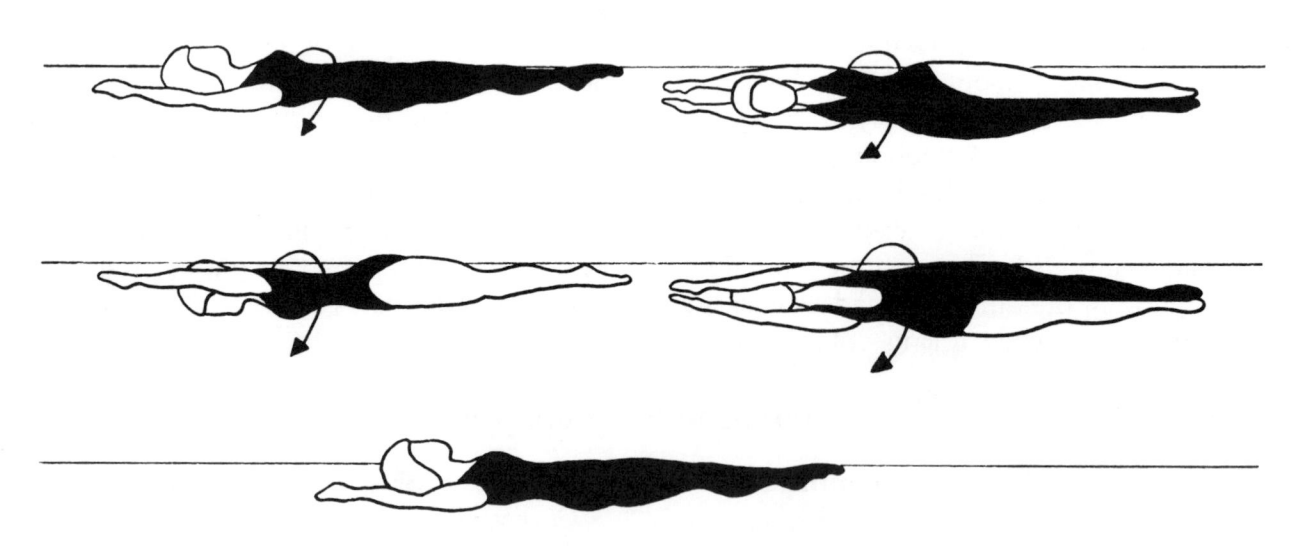

Method of Execution

To perform the Log Roll the swimmer first assumes either a Front or Back Layout position with her hands at her sides. The swimmer initiates the figure by gently sliding her arms up the sides of her body until they are fully extended above her head. At this point the swimmer should press her arms tightly against her ears and stretch her body to its greatest length.

To initiate the roll, the swimmer tightens all the muscles on the side of her body toward which she is going to turn. By lifting one side of her body and pressing down with the other, the swimmer will rotate her body on its longitudinal axis. As in the Corkscrew, the body must rotate as a tight unit. The figure is finished when the swimmer returns to her starting position, whether that was a Front or Back Layout, and gently lowers her arms back to her sides.

Teaching Progression

On the Deck Have the Swimmers:

1. Practice the Back, Front, and Side Layout positions.
2. Practice the layout positions with their arms extended over their heads.
3. Perform the entire Log Roll while standing so that they can get the feel of the movement.

In the Water Have the Swimmers:

1. Practice the Back, Front, and Side Layout positions.
2. Practice the layout positions with their arms extended over their heads.
3. Execute a Breast Stroke followed by a Log Roll. The momentum created by the stroke makes the figure easier to perform and will give the swimmer a feel for the movement in the water.
4. Practice the Log Roll from a stationary position.

Common Errors	Corrections
• Kicking.	• There must not be any kicking. Squeeze the legs tightly together.
• Body arched.	• Do not press the shoulders back. Tighten the abdomen and lift the chest.
• Folding one leg over the other during the roll.	• Squeeze legs tightly together.
• Shoulder rolling before the hip.	• Tighten muscles and rotate the body as a unit.
• Body turning before the head.	• Focus the eyes in the direction in which the body is turning.
• Rolling halfway and not being able to continue.	• Lift one side of the body and press down with the other side.

Somersault, Front Pike

Method of Execution

To perform the Front Pike Somersault, the swimmer first assumes a Front Layout position with her face in the water. She then gets into position for the figure by extending her arms over her head, but keeps her arms under the water. The figure starts as the swimmer moves her trunk down so that her body is in a Front Pike position. To move her trunk, the swimmer presses her shoulders down, leads with the chest, and uses an Alligator scull (or some adaptation of this scull). The arm action will differ among swimmers depending on their body build, buoyancy and personal preferences.

The buttocks, legs, and feet move along the surface as the swimmer pulls her trunk into the Front Pike. When the swimmer's body is at the 90-degree angle, her hips should be where her head began. Light upward muscle tension on the front of the legs will help keep the hips and heels at the surface. When the swimmer reaches the 90-degree Pike, she locks her body in this position. The Pike must be at the hips, not the waist.

To move around in this type of somersault, the swimmer shifts her arms in slow circular pulls until she makes one revolution. As the head and torso surface, the swimmer begins a stationary Canoe scull next to her torso. She keeps her face in the water until her legs and feet return to the surface in a Front Layout position.

Teaching Progression

On the Deck Have the Swimmers:

1. Get a feel for a good Pike position while sitting on the deck.

In the Water Have the Swimmers:

1. Use the sides and bottom of the shallow

end of the pool to practice the four Pike positions illustrated below.

2. Use a flotation device to support their feet while they practice pulling down into the Pike position.

3. Perform a small Breast Stroke and then pull down into the Front Pike. The momentum of the stroke makes it easier to pull the trunk down.

4. Perform the pull-down from a stationary position with a partner helping keep the feet, legs, and hips on the surface. The partner also checks the accuracy of the Pike position.

5. Perform the entire figure.

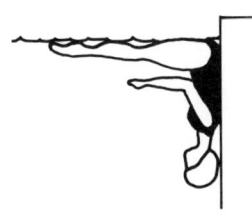

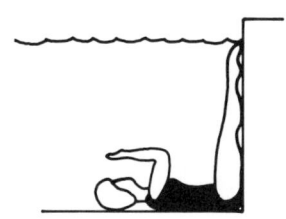

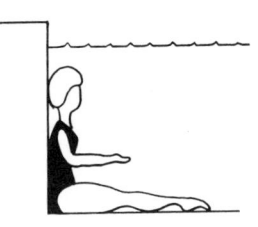

3:00 Position   6:00 Position   9:00 Position   12:00 Position

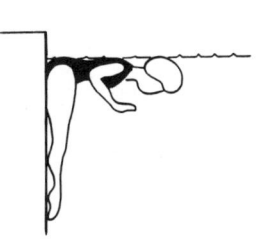

Common Errors

- Feet dropping below the surface as the Pike begins.

- Buttocks popping out of the water as the Pike begins.

- Dropping the head and rounding the shoulders.

- Failure to move forward so that the hips move to a position over the head.

- Overpiking.

Corrections

- Lead with the chest. Press up on the heels and tense the muscles in the front of the legs.

- Do not begin the Pike until forward movement starts. Make sure that the arm pull is deep enough so that the body pikes from the hips, not from the waist. Push back on the shoulders and lead with the chest.

- Push back on the shoulders and keep the head in line with the trunk. Lead with the chest.

- Stretch into the pull-down. While learning use a small Breast Stroke before starting the downward movement.

- Push back on shoulders and head. Lead with the chest. Try to arch the back slightly while piking.

Jumpover

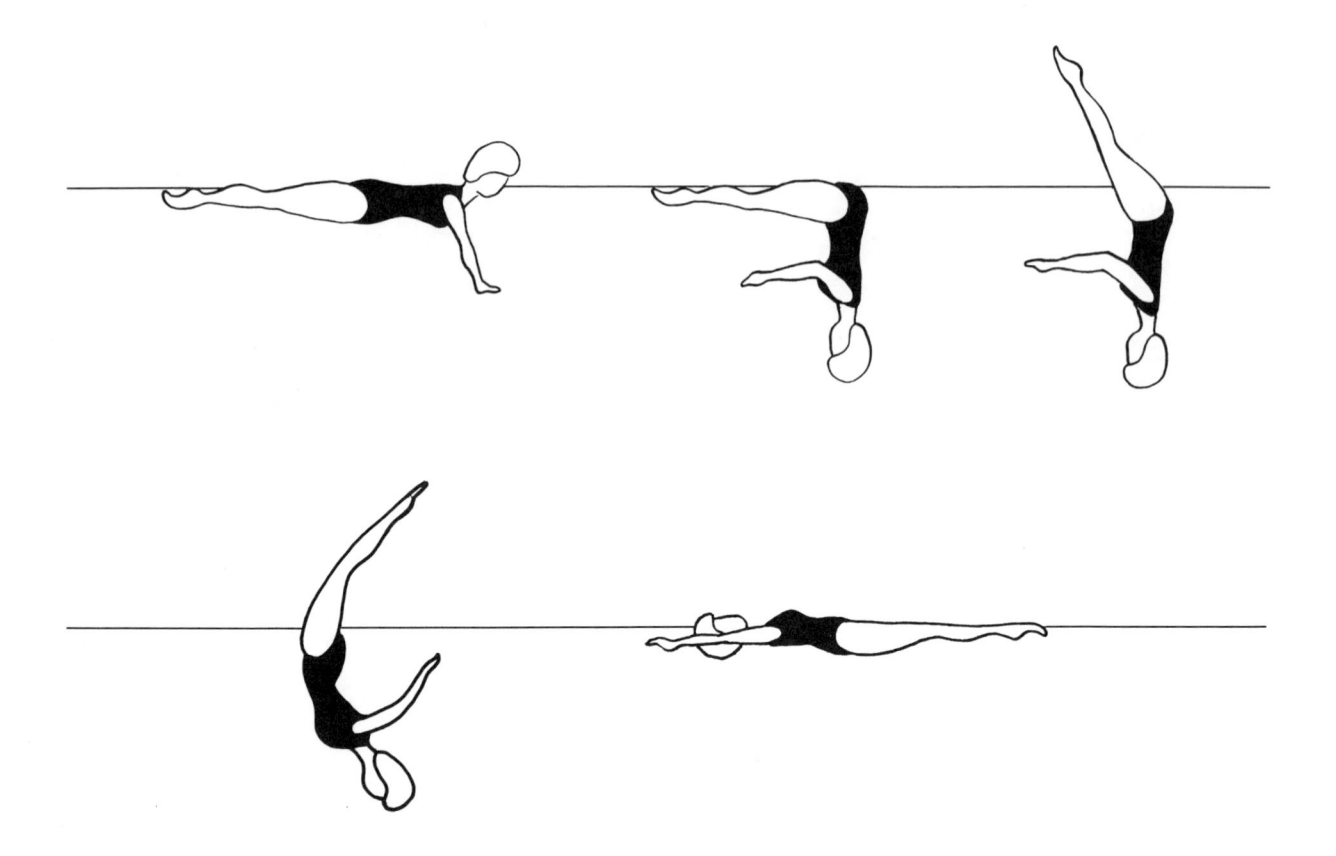

Method of Execution

To perform the Jumpover the swimmer first assumes a Front Layout position. She then pulls down into a Front Pike, as in the Front Pike Somersault. From the 3 o'clock Front Pike position, the swimmer lifts both legs together in an arc over the surface. To perform the leg movement, the swimmer places her hands just under her knees with the palms facing down and presses the hands straight toward the bottom of the pool while moving the legs over the water. The swimmer should squeeze her legs together and keep them fully extended throughout the movement.

As the legs describe the arc, the body moves from the Pike to an arched position. Once the legs have moved over the hips and are descending toward the water, the swimmer performs a Torpedo scull to bring the trunk toward the surface. The feet should stay on top of the water while the body gradually assumes a Back Layout position from the arched position, with the arms overhead.

Teaching Progression

In the Water Have the Swimmers:

1. Assume the Front Pike position in shallow water with their hands on the bottom of the pool. Direct them to practice lifting their legs in an arc over the surface. They must be certain that their legs are squeezed together and don't come apart. Once the legs have begun their descent, the swimmers should push off from the pool with their hands to initiate a Torpedo scull up to the surface.

2. Practice the figure in deep water.

Common Errors	Corrections
• Feet and legs coming apart during the lift.	• Squeeze legs together tightly.
• Not getting legs lifted out of the water.	• Check hand positions. Palms should face the bottom of the pool. Tighten the buttocks while lifting the legs.
• Feet sinking after the arc.	• Press up on the toes.
• Body not surfacing to the Back Layout position.	• Bring the chin forward slightly until the face comes out of the water.

SEQUENCE 2

"California Girls" by the Beach Boys

In the second sequence the swimmer uses all of the skills learned in Unit II, plus several of the skills learned in Unit I. As with the sequence in Unit I, each movement that the swimmer needs to perform is charted below. The method of teaching the sequence should be the same as that discussed in Unit I.

The movements choreographed in this sequence take the swimmer through the first three measures of the music. The swimmer can repeat these movements as the music continues in order to practice the entire routine again. Once she learns the sequence, the swimmer may want to try choreographing some additional measures and incorporating more of the skills she learned in Unit I.

SEQUENCE 2
Music: "California Girls" by the Beach Boys

Measures	Beats: 1	2	3	4
Introduction	X X	X X	X X	X X
1	Right side scissors kick	Left Back Stroke	Left side scissors kick	Right Back Stroke
2	Right side scissors kick	Left Back Stroke	Left side scissors kick	Right Back Stroke —leave arm overhead
3	Corkscrew to right	⟶		Back Layout
4	Left Back Stroke —leave arm overhead	Right Back Stroke —leave arm overhead	Roll onto stomach	⟶
5	Breast Stroke pull	Breast Stroke kick	Breast Stroke pull	Breast Stroke kick
	Somersault, Front Pike:			
6	Front Pike pull-down	to 3:00 o'clock position	Scull around to	6:00 o'clock position
7	Scull around to	9:00 o'clock position	Scull around to	Front Layout
8	Breast Stroke pull	Breast Stroke kick	Breast Stroke pull	Breast Stroke kick
	Jumpover:			
9	Front Pike pull-down	to 3:00 o'clock position	Lift legs in arc over the water	⟶
10	Arch over	⟶	Torpedo scull up to Back Layout	⟶
11	Torpedo scull			⟶
12	Oyster		⟶	Surface and smile!

UNIT III

Unit III Skill Performance Objectives

Swimmers should be able to perform the following skills for the designated distances or in the designated way.

Strokes and Transitions:

Side Flutter Kick and Variations—25 yards

Basic Positions and Sculls:

Reverse Torpedo Scull—15 yards

Bent Knee Position Scull, Supine—10 yards each leg

Bent Knee Position Scull, Prone—10 yards each leg

Figures:

Shark Circle—One each direction

Marlin—One each direction

Somersault, Back Pike

Dolphin, Head-First

Sequence:

Performed to "Lemon Tree" by Will Holt

Side Flutter Kick and Variations

Body Position

- Body extended in a Side Layout position.
- Lower arm overhead and underneath the water.
- Upper arm along the side of the body and upper leg.
- Body slanted toward the feet slightly to keep the kick underwater.

Method of Execution

The swimmer should find a balance point with her body almost horizontal in the Side Layout position. She rests her lower ear on her lower arm, turning her head enough to allow for easy breathing.

The kick goes from side to side, parallel to the surface. The swimmer executes the kick both in front of and behind the body, not just to one side or the other. The kick starts from the hips, and the legs stay relaxed in order to provide a smooth, fluid kick.

Uses for the Side Flutter Kick

Once the swimmer masters the Side Flutter kick, she can combine it with the arm movements of many strokes. For example, she can start with a Side Stroke, begin the kick, and have the upper arm perform a stroke variation which moves the swimmer onto her back. The swimmer continues the kick while she is on her back. She can then roll onto the other side, continuing the kick, and perform a Side Stroke on this side, or continue the roll and move into a Breast Stroke. The Side Flutter provides the swimmer with endless opportunities to use creative arm movements while the legs propel the body through the water.

Common Errors

- Tipping onto the back.
- Tipping onto the front.
- Splashing during the kick.

Corrections

- Roll toward the stomach.
- Roll toward the back.
- Check for a good Side Layout position, with the body slanted down slightly toward the feet.

Common Errors (cont.)	Corrections (cont.)
• Not swimming in a straight line.	• Check lower arm placement. The body will travel in the direction that the lower arm is pointing. Check to make sure the legs kick an even distance in front of and behind the line of the body.
• Sinking while creating new arm strokes.	• Kick harder. Make sure the lower ear is resting on the lower arm.

Reverse Torpedo Scull

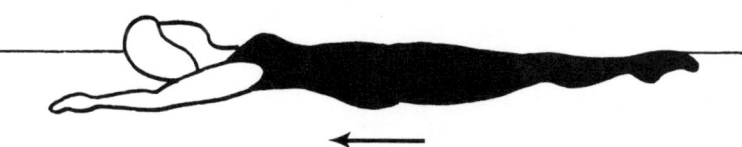

Scull Position and Direction of Movement

- Body extended in a Back Layout position.
- Arms extended overhead.
- Head and shoulders in line with the body.
- Face, hips, thighs, and feet at the surface.
- Swimmer moves head-first.

Method of Execution

From a Back Layout position, the swimmer gently slides her arms up the sides of her body to a position overhead. She must make sure to move her arms gently enough so that she doesn't move foot-first. She flexes her wrists sharply and turns her palms outward, facing away from her body. She bends her elbows slightly, which makes her hands almost touch. She should not cup her hands.

Just as in the Alligator scull, the swimmer leads with her fingertips and sweeps her hands out from her body about 12 inches by extending her elbows. Without pausing, she then rotates her hands so that the palms face inward, and she sweeps the hands back toward each other by bending the elbows. At the end of this sweep the hands will almost touch again. The movement of the hands as they go back and forth should resemble a figure eight. The swimmer must keep her fingers and thumb close together in order to exert maximum pressure on the water, but keep the wrists and elbows relaxed to ensure a smooth sweeping motion.

Coaching Tip: Have the swimmers imagine they are smoothing sand to develop the proper hand motion.

Teaching Progression

On the Deck Have the Swimmers:

1. Stand with their arms extended overhead. Direct them to flex their wrists sharply, turning their palms out so that their little fingers are pressed toward their heads and their thumbs are lifted. From this position, the swimmers should sweep their hands out about 12 inches by extending the elbows and leading with the fingertips. At the end of the sweep, the swimmers are to rotate their hands so that the palms face each other, and press down with their thumbs while lifting the little fingers. Then have them sweep their hands back by bending the elbows, still with the fingertips leading. Have the swimmers continue the movement slowly. Emphasize the hand rotation at the end of each sweep and the constant wrist flexion.

In the Water Have the Swimmers:

1. Practice the sculling movement while a partner supports the torso. Use the cues "rotate out," "sweep out," "rotate in," and "sweep in."
2. Practice in the Back Layout position with their feet supported by an inner tube or some other flotation device. Continue to use cues. The swimmers should be concentrating totally on their hand movements.
3. Practice in the proper position, with the cues "sweep" and "rotate."
4. Take a deep breath and start the Reverse Torpedo movement with the body under the water. As their bodies surface, the swimmers should raise their chests and tighten their stomach muscles in order to stay on top of the water. Beginning synchro swimmers may submerge their head and shoulders so that they can watch their arms and hands perform the scull.
5. Speed up the motion as they learn it.
6. Start with the Alligator scull in a Front Layout position. While keeping the arms overhead, they should perform a Log Roll onto their backs and continue sculling. The sculling motion will remain the same throughout since the same sculling techniques are used in the Reverse Torpedo and Alligator sculls.

Common Errors

- Rather than an equally strong inward and outward sweep, the inward movement becomes only a resting (recovery) movement. This is finning, not sculling.
- Fingers separate.
- Stiff, rigid wrists and elbows.

Corrections

- Use the cue words "sweep" and "rotate."

- Close fingers.
- Relax; lead with the fingertips; "Smooth sand."

Common Errors (cont.)	Corrections (cont.)
• Movement initiated primarily from the shoulders.	• Initiate movement from elbows as much as possible.
• Feet and hips sinking.	• Lift feet to the surface. Tighten stomach muscles and loosen buttock muscles. Don't arch the back. Learn the scull with the head and shoulders submerged.
• Failure to maintain wrist flexion, especially on inward sweep.	• Flex wrists sharply. Hands should feel like hooks on the ends of the arms. Keep the palms facing toward the body.
• Body doesn't move head-first.	• Not enough wrist flexion. Swimmer may be flexing only the fingers instead of the wrists.
• Failure to extend ankles and toes.	• Extend ankles and point toes.
• Hands break the surface.	• Scull deeper.
• Sweeping the hands too far from the body.	• Don't sweep outward more than about 12 inches.
• Lifting the head.	• Press head and shoulders back. The swimmer can learn the scull with the head and shoulders submerged.
• Failure to lead with the fingertips.	• Always remember to rotate the wrist and it will be in the correct position to lead.

Bent Knee Position Scull, Supine

Supine Bent Knee Position

- Body extended in a Back Layout (supine) position.

- One knee bent with the thigh perpendicular to the surface. The foot of the bent knee is on the inside of the extended leg's knee.

- Hips and the thigh and front of the extended leg are as close to the surface as possible. The face is out of the water.

Method of Execution

The swimmer first assumes a Back Layout position with her face out of the water and her hips, thighs, and feet at the surface. If the swimmer wants to remain stationary or move head-first as she moves into the position, she uses the arm movement of the Eel scull with her palms facing either the bottom of the pool or her feet, respectively. If she wants to move foot-first, the swimmer uses the arm movement of the Snail scull.

To get into the Bent Knee position, the swimmer slowly draws her right foot along the inside of the left leg until the right thigh is perpendicular to the surface. When the thigh is perpendicular, the right heel should be at or above the knee of the other leg. The foot of the extended leg should remain at the surface and the ankles and toes of both feet should be fully extended.

As the swimmer begins to draw the knee up, the hips will drop sharply. By lifting the chest, pressing the shoulders back, and tightening the abdominal and buttock muscles, the swimmer will be able to keep the hips closer to the surface. The sculling action should also be increased. The swimmer must be careful to keep her hands near her hips and below the surface.

The swimmer then returns the bent leg to its original position by slowly sliding the foot along the inside of the extended leg. After both legs are extended, the swimmer starts drawing the left leg into the bent position and leaves the right leg straight. Alternating the legs is called "marching."

Teaching Progression

On the Deck Have the Swimmers:

1. Assume a Back Layout position. The swimmers can get the feel of the abdominal and buttock muscles tightening by lifting their heads and legs about two inches off the deck. From this position, they should move slowly into the Bent Knee position, return the leg to the extended position, and move the other leg into the Bent Knee position.

In the Water Have the Swimmers:

1. Either support the foot of the extended leg on the pool gutter or have a partner hold it while they assume the Bent Knee position.

2. Practice with the foot of the extended leg supported by a flotation device.

3. Sit in the water in the Bent Knee position. Their hips and bent knee will be low and almost totally submerged. The swimmers should then tighten the abdomen and buttocks, stretch the body, and press the chest up. They will have to scull hard to lift the bent knee out of the water.

4. Practice the Bent Knee position in a stationary position.

5. Practice the Bent Knee Position scull moving head-first.

6. Practice the Bent Knee Position scull moving foot-first.

Common Errors	Corrections
• Failure to keep the foot of the extended leg at the surface.	• Lift upward on the foot while pressing the head and shoulders back.
• Scull deteriorates to a grabbing action as the knee bends.	• Maintain a strong sculling motion.
• Placing the foot of the bent leg on top of the extended leg.	• Place the foot alongside the extended leg.
• Failure to keep the thigh of the bent knee perpendicular to the water.	• Push the knee away from the chest and push the shoulders back.

Bent Knee Position Scull, Prone

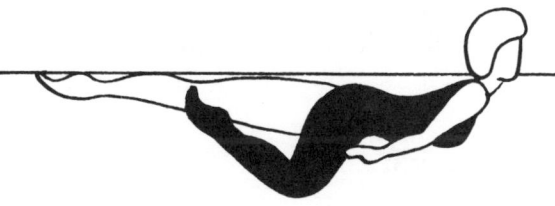

Prone Bent Knee Position

- Body extended in a Front Layout (prone) position.
- One knee bent with the thigh perpendicular to the body and the surface. The foot of the bent knee is on the inside of the extended leg at or above the knee.
- Body arched slightly. The head, buttocks, and heels are at the surface. The face may be in or out of the water.

Method of Execution

The swimmer first assumes a Front Layout position. Her head, buttocks, and heels are at the surface. Her face may be in or out of the water. If the swimmer wants to remain stationary or move head-first, she uses the arm movement of the Canoe scull.

To get into the Bent Knee position, the swimmer slowly draws her right foot along the inside of the left leg until the right thigh is perpendicular to the body. When the thigh is perpendicular, the toes of the right foot should be at or above the knee of the other leg. The heel of the extended leg should remain at the surface, and the ankles and toes of both feet should be fully extended.

As the swimmer begins to draw the knee up, the hips may drop and the back may arch. The swimmer needs to tighten the abdominal and buttock muscles to keep the hips up. She should also increase the sculling action as the knee bends. The swimmer must be careful to keep her hands near her hips and below the surface.

The swimmer then returns the bent leg to its original position by slowly sliding the foot along the inside of the extended leg. After both legs are extended, the swimmer starts drawing the left leg into the bent position and leaves the right leg straight.

Teaching Progression

On the Deck Have the Swimmers:

1. Assume a Front Layout position on a bench, with their legs extending over the edge. They should lift their head and chest, arching the upper back as necessary. From this position, they are to move slowly into the Bent Knee position, return the leg to the extended position, and move the other leg into the Bent Knee position.

In the Water Have the Swimmers:

1. Either support the foot of the extended leg on the pool gutter or have a partner hold it while they assume the Bent Knee position.

2. Practice with the foot of the extended leg supported by a flotation device.

3. Practice the correct technique in a stationary position.

4. Practice getting into the Bent Knee position moving head-first.

Common Errors

- Extended leg and hips sinking as the swimmer bends her knee.

- Scull deteriorates to a grabbing action as the knee bends.

- Curling the foot of the bent leg on top of the extended leg.

- Failure to keep the thigh of the bent knee perpendicular to the body and the water.

Corrections

- Press up with the heel and down on the shoulders. Putting the face in the water will make the position a little easier.

- Maintain a strong sculling motion.

- Place the foot alongside the extended leg.

- Push the knee away from the chest and lean forward in the water.

Shark Circle

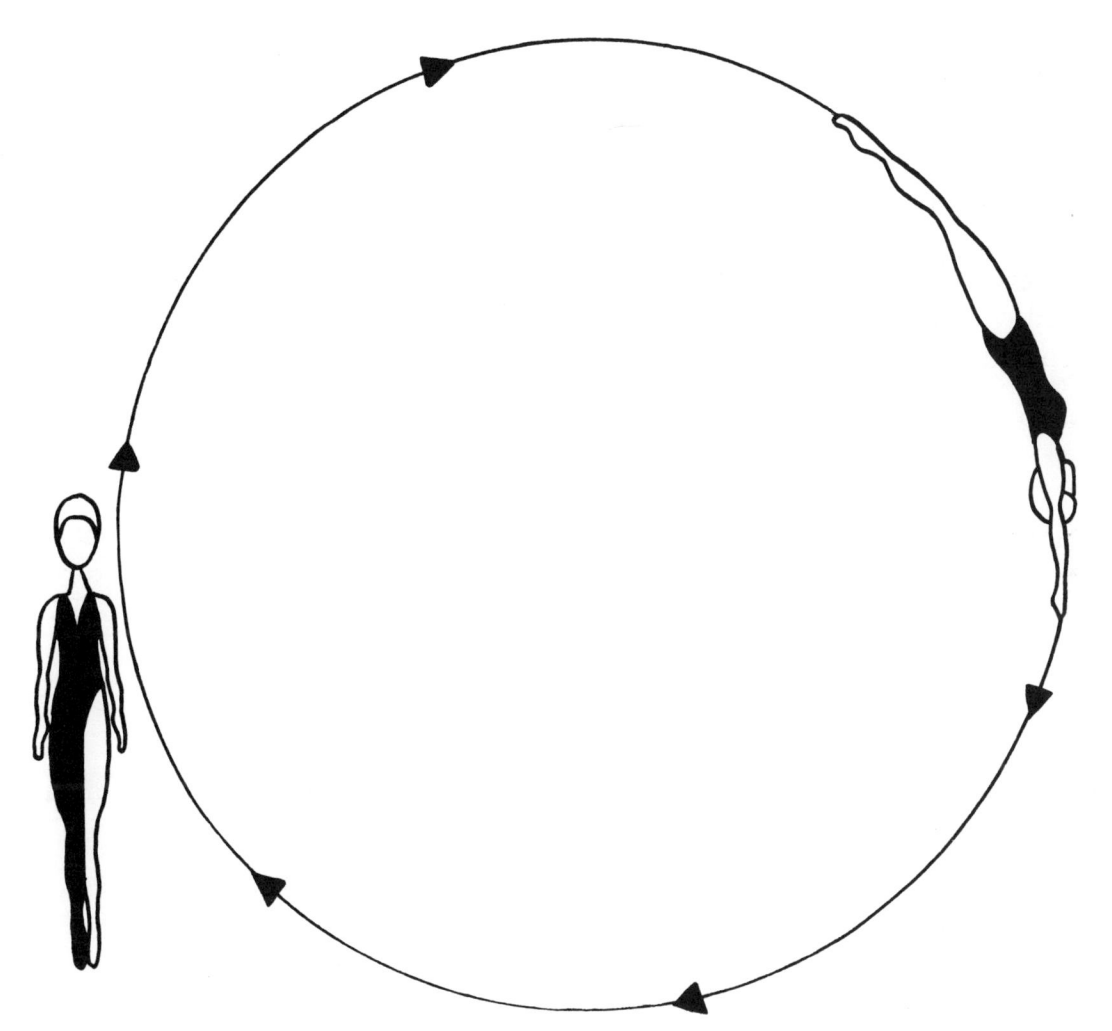

Overhead view of Shark Circle

Method of Execution

The swimmer assumes a Back Layout position and begins the figure by rotating into a Side Layout position. The swimmer then arches her body and extends her top arm over her head, which will cause her head to submerge. Pressing the extended arm against the head will help keep the head, hip, calf, thigh, and feet at the surface.

To initiate the circular movement, the swimmer uses an Eel scull action with the lower arm, with the fingertips pointing toward the bottom of the pool. The legs must remain still throughout. The swimmer should keep the scull beneath the hips to help support them. The body will travel in a circle described by the arch in the swimmer's back. When the swimmer completes a full circle, she rotates back to the Back Layout position.

Teaching Progression

On the Deck Have the Swimmers:

1. Practice rotating from the Back Layout to the Side Layout position. Have them arch their backs and extend the top arm.

In the Water Have the Swimmers:

1. Support their feet on the pool gutter and practice the Side Layout position with their backs arched and the top arm extended.

2. Support their feet in a flotation device and practice sculling in the Side Layout position. They should concentrate on the arm action.

3. Execute a small Side Stroke followed by a Shark Circle. The momentum of the stroke will help keep the body on top of the water during the Circle.

4. Practice the correct technique.

Common Errors

- Failure to keep the legs and feet at the surface.

- Kicking.

- Pulling with a modified Side Stroke instead of sculling.

- Rather than an equally strong inward and outward sweep, the inward movement becomes only a resting (recovery) movement. This is finning, not sculling.

- Bending the knees while in the Side Layout.

Corrections

- Press feet up on the surface and keep the head in line with the body. Stretch the extended arm and press it against the head.

- Squeeze the legs and feet tightly together.

- Maintain correct sculling technique.

- Use the cue words "sweep" and "rotate."

- Lock the knees and arch the lower back.

Marlin

View of Marlin from overhead

Method of Execution

To perform the Marlin the swimmer first assumes a Back Layout position. Her arms should be extended at right angles to her body, straight from her shoulders, and her palms should face toward her feet. The motion starts with the swimmer extending her right arm over her head while moving the left arm down to the side of her body. Simultaneously, the swimmer rotates to her right into a Side Layout position. When she is in the Side Layout position, her right arm should be extended overhead and her left arm should be extended by her side. The swimmer continues to rotate into a Front Layout position and at the same time brings her arms back to form right angles from her sides.

The swimmer then continues to rotate into a Side Layout position on her left side while extending her left arm over her head and the right arm down to the side of her body. In the Side Layout, her left arm should be extended overhead and her right arm should be extended by her side. The rotation continues back to the Back Layout as the swimmer moves her arms back to their initial position, perpendicular to her sides.

The swimmer should keep the movement smooth and continuous rather than stopping as she reaches each layout position.

As the arms move from position to position, they must stay completely extended and just below the surface. If the swimmer performs the figure correctly, the arms will always be directly opposite one another. Because of the movement of the arms, by the time the swimmer performs one complete rotation, she will have executed a quarter-turn around the vertical axis running through her body at the hips.

Teaching Progression

In the Water Have the Swimmers:

1. Practice the figure by imitating someone perform it who is standing on the deck. Swimmers should learn the figure with their legs extended and their face in the water. Keeping the face in the water helps keep the feet at the surface.

Coaching Tip: Have the swimmers learn to do the figure by positioning themselves so that they can easily observe when they have completed a quarter-turn. If the swimmers observe the lines on the bottom of the pool, they will be able to orient themselves when they are in the Front Layout position.

2. Perform the Marlin in the Bent Knee position once they master the figure with the legs extended.

Common Errors	Corrections
• Sculling to assist in turning or to keep the feet at the surface.	• Correct arm action will make sculling unnecessary. Keep the head and shoulders in line with the body, keep the face in the water, and lift the heels to keep the feet at the surface.
• Bending the elbows.	• Keep elbows locked and arms fully extended.
• Moving one arm before the other.	• Arms should move in exact opposition to one another.
• Failure to execute the quarter-turn.	• As the body rolls into a Front Layout position, use the lane lines to orient the position. If the body angle is inaccurate, exert more or less pull with the arms when completing the action.

Somersault, Back Pike

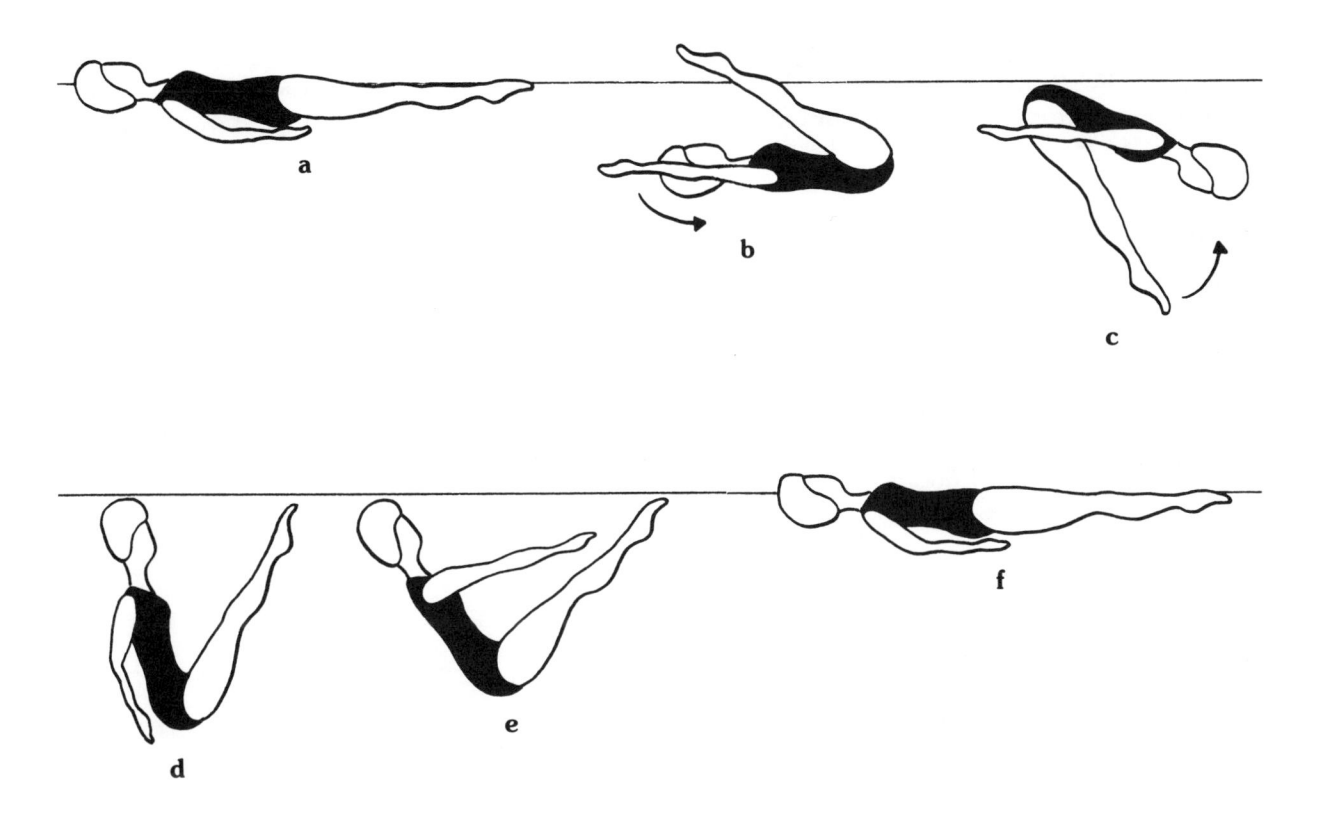

Method of Execution

The swimmer first assumes a Back Layout position. She performs a Back Pike by lifting her legs up and over the water toward her head. While lifting her legs, she rotates her hands so that the palms face the surface. Then, with the thumbs leading, she slices through the water back toward the shoulders at a slight downward angle. Her buttocks should remain close to the surface as she assumes the Back Pike position.

After the swimmer is in the Back Pike, she begins to somersault by performing a circular sculling action with her arms without breaking the surface of the water. The somersault should be a slow, continuous motion around an axis between the trunk and the legs. The swimmer must concentrate on keeping her legs extended and pressed forward to maintain as tight a pike as possible.

The momentum created by bringing the legs into the Back Pike will move the body until the toes point toward the bottom of the pool. The rest of the rotation is accomplished by sculling at the hips. While the body rotates, the buttocks, back, and head should pass just beneath the surface.

When the swimmer finishes the rotation and her head and feet are just below the surface, she extends her body slowly, allowing her head and feet to emerge simultaneously and allowing her hips to rise. She completes the figure by resuming a Back Layout position.

Teaching Progression

On the Deck Have the Swimmers:

1. Practice the Back Pike position while lying on the deck. They should press their legs as far over their heads as possible without rounding their shoulders (see Figure b).

In the Water Have the Swimmers:

1. Assume the Back Layout position and practice just the arm movement which occurs as they bring their legs into the pike. (The legs should remain horizontal.)

2. Assume a Back Layout position with their feet supported on the pool gutter. Have a partner lift the swimmer's legs and help her bring them over her head into the Back Pike position.

3. Practice the first portion of the figure from the Back Layout until their toes are pointing toward the pool bottom (see Figures a-c).

4. Practice from the middle of the figure, where the toes are pointing toward the pool bottom, until they resume the Back Layout position (see Figures c-f).

5. Practice the entire figure.

Common Errors

- Failure to lift the legs up and over the surface. The body pikes and "Oysters," then the legs are pushed back over the head.

- As the legs reach the surface over the head, there is a hesitation in the backward rotation.

- Body is too deep or too shallow during the somersault.

- At the conclusion of the somersault, the head appears before the feet.

- The head presses forward, rounding the shoulders.

Corrections

- Emphasize *lifting* the legs. Hands should press flat toward the shoulders. Don't drop hands to the hips and then push up.

- Keep pressing toward the body with the ankles and knees, and away from the legs with the buttocks and thighs.

- Control the depth with sculling.

- Keep the pike tight. If the swimmer is buoyant, she should scull by pushing toward the surface.

- Press the head and shoulders back.

Dolphin, Head-First

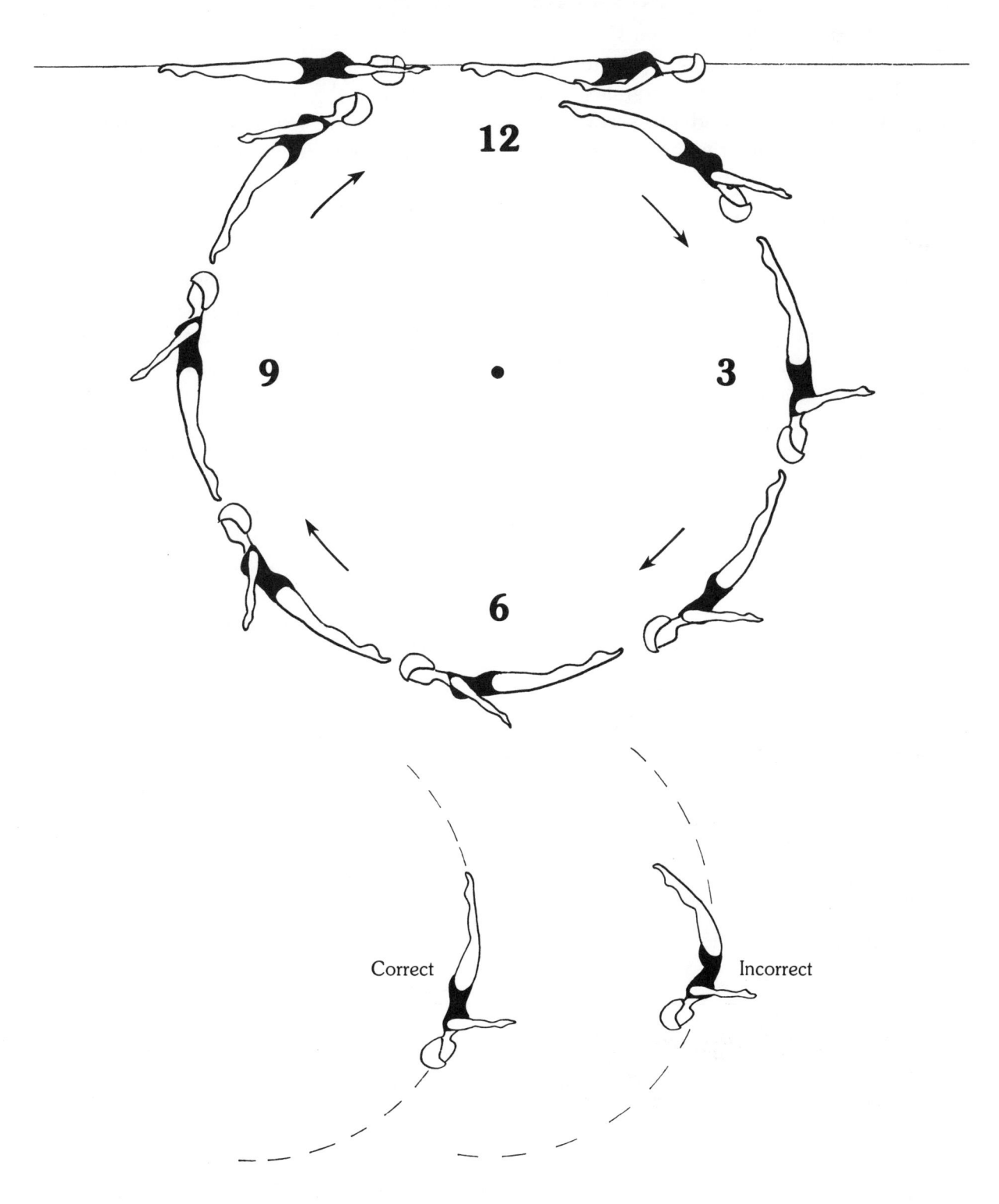

Correct   Incorrect

Method of Execution

To perform the Dolphin the swimmer first assumes a Back Layout. She gets ready to move through the figure by gently sliding her hands up the sides of her body and over her head. The swimmer uses a Reverse Torpedo scull to move her body head-first. She gently arches her upper back and presses her shoulders down while keeping her head in line with her shoulders. When she does this, her head and shoulders will enter the water. The swimmer must be careful to perform this move gently and not throw her head back. She should press her heels up so that her feet remain on the surface.

The body will begin to describe a circle under the water. If the circle were thought of as a clock face, 12 o'clock would be at the surface, 3 o'clock would be the side the swimmer passed with her head pointed down, 6 o'clock would be the part of the circle closest to the bottom of the pool, and 9 o'clock would be the side the swimmer passed with her head pointed toward the surface. As the swimmer reaches 4 o'clock, she gradually moves her hands back toward her sides and begins to use a Canoe scull. When the body reaches the 8 o'clock position, the swimmer's buoyancy will raise her body to the surface. In order not to ascend too rapidly, she will have to scull by pushing toward the surface. As her head begins to emerge from the water, the swimmer turns her hands over. The palms face down and the fingertips point toward the feet as the body surfaces. The figure concludes with the swimmer resuming a Back Layout position.

Throughout the Dolphin, the swimmer must keep her body extended and slightly arched as in the Circle position described on page 12. The circle her body follows should have a diameter one-and-a-half times her height, or about eight feet. During the Dolphin the swimmer's back should remain parallel to the horizontal axis around which she is rotating and her head, buttocks, and feet should stay on the imaginary line of the circle.

Teaching Progression

In the Water Have the Swimmers:

1. Start by facing the side of the pool and gripping the gutter firmly with both hands. Direct them to press their feet against the side with their knees bent and near their chests. The swimmers should then push off hard and arch their backs while extending their arms overhead. They must then pull their bodies around in a circle by grabbing the water overhead.

2. Gently press back on their shoulders without arching their backs and perform a Reverse Torpedo scull. This will allow the swimmers to watch their hands while they practice a Reverse Torpedo.

3. Practice the complete Dolphin.

Common Errors

- Turning sideways.

- Pivoting around the legs or the head instead of moving along the circumference, or moving the head and buttocks along the circumference but not the legs.

- Feet sinking as the head starts descending.

Corrections

- Make sure to pull both arms evenly and not to roll the body to either side.

- Initiate backward movement before starting the descent and continue to move backward during the first quarter of the circle. Loosen the arch in the back.

- Don't arch the lower back. Lift the feet.

Common Errors (cont.)

- Feet drifting up as the head surfaces at the end of the Dolphin.

- Incorrectly shaped circle.

Corrections (cont.)

- As the head surfaces, press down hard on the feet. Allow them to surface gradually as the body continues the head-first motion.

- Review "Method of Execution."

SEQUENCE 3

"Lemon Tree" by Will Holt

In the third sequence the swimmers use all the skills learned in Unit III, plus several of the skills learned in the first two units. As in previous units, the movements are charted below. The method for teaching the sequence should follow the method discussed in Unit I.

The movements choreographed in this sequence take the swimmer through the first 23 measures of the music. The swimmer can repeat these movements as the music continues in order to practice the entire routine again. Once she learns this set of movements, the swimmer should start choreographing some additional measures by combining strokes, figures and propulsions in creative ways. This will help prepare her to choreograph her own sequences in later units.

SEQUENCE 3
Music: "Lemon Tree" by Will Holt

Measures	Beats: 1	2	3	4
	Side flutter on left side:			
1	Right arm up	Arm down	Right arm up	Right Back Stroke
2	Right Side Stroke pull	Scissor kick	Right Side Stroke pull	Scissor kick
	Side flutter on right side:			
3	Left arm up	Arm down	Left arm up	Left Back Stroke
4	Left Side Stroke pull	Scissor kick	Roll onto back	Back Layout

Sequence 3 (cont.)

		Marching:			
5		Right Bent Knee	Switch to left Bent Knee	Switch to right Bent Knee	Back Layout
6		Left Bent Knee	Switch to right Bent Knee	Switch to left Bent Knee	Back Layout
		Somersault, Back Pike:			
7		Pike legs overhead	Somersault in one revolution	————————————————→	
8		————————————————————————→		Surface to Back Layout	————→
9		Eel scull, traveling	————————————————————————————→		
		Marlin:			
10		Back Layout	1/8 turn to Front Layout	————————→	1/8 turn to Back Layout
11		Right Side Stroke pull	Scissor kick	Extend left arm overhead as face goes under water	Shark Circle
12		————————————————————————————————————→			
13		————————————————————————————→			Back Layout, —leave left arm overhead
14		Right Back Stroke —leave arm overhead	Reverse Torpedo	————————→	Dolphin, Head-First
15		————————————————————————————————————→			
16		————————————————————————————————————→			
17		Surface to Back Layout	Back Layout	Eel scull, traveling	————→
		Back Flutter Kick:			
18		Right arm up	Arm down	Right Back Stroke	Roll onto stomach on right arm.
19		Breast Stroke pull	Breast Stroke kick	Breast Stroke pull	Breast Stroke kick
		Jumpover:			
20		Front Pike pull-down	to 3:00 o'clock position	Lift legs in arc over the water	————→
21		Arch over	————————→	Torpedo scull up	to back layout
22		Roll onto stomach	from Torpedo scull	Bend knees to get	legs under hips
23		Lift left arm up	Sink (submerge smiling)	————————————————→	

UNIT IV

Unit IV Skill Performance Objectives

Swimmers should be able to perform the following skills for the designated distances or times, or in the designated way.

Strokes and Transitions:

Eggbeater Kick, Stationary—30 seconds

Basic Positions and Sculls:

Lobster Scull—15 yards

Vertical Tuck Position

Inverted Split Position with Support Scull

Figures:

Ballet Leg, Single and Alternate

Walkover, Front

Dolphin, Bent Knee

Porpoise

Sequence:

Performed to "Fiddler on the Roof" by Jerry Bock

Eggbeater Kick, Stationary

The Eggbeater method of treading water provides continuous support for the swimmer because there is no resting phase for the legs. Swimmers can use the kick to maintain a high vertical trunk position or to propel themselves while in a vertical position. They can also use the Eggbeater for transitions from a vertical position to a horizontal position or vice versa. While the legs kick, the arms are free to create various movements.

Method of Execution

The swimmer performs the Eggbeater kick in an erect sitting position. Her back should be straight and perpendicular to the water, with the neck extended and the shoulders down and relaxed. The knees should be in the same horizontal plane as the hips so that the upper thighs form a 90-degree angle with the trunk. The lower legs hang down from the knees toward the pool bottom so that they form a 90-degree angle with the thighs.

With the knees spread apart as far as possible, the swimmer performs a Breast Stroke kick with one leg by making as large a circle as possible with the foot and lower leg. She should reach as far as she can forward, sideways, and backward, while still maintaining the 90-degree angle between her thighs and trunk. As the foot moves sideways and forward, the ankles and toes flex sharply, and as the foot moves backward, they extend sharply. As soon as one leg completes the circle, the other leg begins. The left leg moves clockwise and the right leg moves counterclockwise.

All the movement should be confined to the leg area between the knees and the toes. The rest of the body should remain stationary.

Teaching Progression

On the Deck Have the Swimmers:

1. Sit on the edge of the pool, a chair, or a diving board and practice the movement slowly with one leg at a time. They should concentrate on making a large circle with the lower leg and on proper flexion and extension of the ankles and toes.

2. Move the legs alternately, progressively getting faster.

In the Water Have the Swimmers:

1. Place their backs against the side of the pool. They should support themselves with their elbows on the gutter and practice the movement with each leg separately and then both together. The kick should start very slow as the swimmers concentrate on proper technique, but it should get progressively faster.

2. Use a kickboard or inner tube under each arm for support and practice the kick.

3. Practice the kick in a Front Layout position. They should clasp their hands behind their back and keep their head and chin out of the water. Swimmers should concentrate on making sure their toes are turned out and their heels are turned in.

4. Practice the kick while using a sculling motion with their arms to help support the body.

5. Practice the Eggbeater kick without support.

Common Errors

- Failure to maintain a proper sitting position.

- Failure to keep the feet in one horizontal plane.

- Failure to keep the knees spread wide.

- Failure to trace large circles with the feet.

- Failure to maintain a straight back, extended neck, and relaxed shoulders.

- Keeping toes pointed throughout the entire kick.

Corrections

- Don't allow the knees and hips to drop; keep them flexed sharply.

- Trace a circle with the feet about the same depth in the water at all times.

- Spread the knees wide to keep the base of the support wide and thus make it easier to stay high.

- Don't allow the circle to be "cut off," especially at the sides.

- Don't lean forward or hunch the shoulders. Lean back and lift the chin high.

- This is one skill in synchro that requires flexed feet!

Lobster Scull

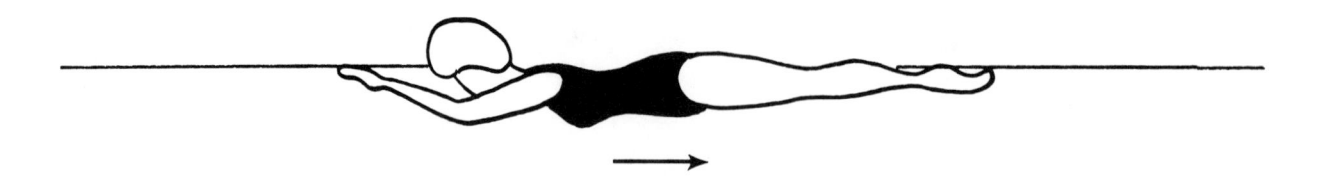

Scull Position and Direction of Movement

- Body extended in Front Layout position with the arms above the head.
- Lower back slightly arched. Head, buttocks, and heels are at the surface.
- Face in or out of the water.
- Body moves in a foot-first direction.

Method of Execution

The swimmer gets into a Front Layout position and gently slides her arms up the sides of her body to an extended position overhead. She hyperextends her wrists sharply and turns her palms outward, facing away from her body, with her fingertips pointing up. Her elbows should be bent slightly so that the hands are almost touching.

Just as in the Eel, the swimmer leads with her wrists, pressing her palms out away from the body in a 12-inch sweep by extending her elbows. Without pausing, she then rotates her hands so that the palms face inward and sweeps the hands back toward each other by bending the elbows. The wrists continue to lead the movement, and the wrists remain hyperextended. The movement of the hands as they go back and forth should resemble a figure eight. The swimmer must keep her fingers and thumb close together in order to exert maximum pressure on the water, but keep the wrists and elbows relaxed to ensure a smooth sweeping motion.

Coaching Tip: Have the swimmers imagine they are smoothing sand to develop the proper hand motion.

The swimmer maintains the arched position by pressing up with her heels and slightly down with her shoulders. This will keep her horizontal in the water.

Teaching Progression

On the Deck Have the Swimmers:

1. Stand with their arms extended overhead. Direct them to hyperextend their wrists sharply and angle their palms out. They should then lift their little fingers and press the thumbs down toward the head as they sweep their hands outward about 12 inches, leading with the wrists by extending their elbows. At the end of the sweep, the swimmers are to

rotate their hands so that the palms face each other, with the thumbs lifted and the little fingers pressed down toward the head. Then the hands are swept back inward by bending the elbows, still with the wrists leading. Have the swimmers continue the movement slowly. Emphasize the hand rotation at the end of each sweep and the constant wrist hyperextension.

In the Water Have the Swimmers:
1. Practice the movement in a Front Layout position with their feet hooked over the edge of the pool gutter. Have them execute the sculling action slowly while you cue them with "rotate outward, sweep outward" and "rotate inward, sweep inward." Emphasize wrist hyperextension throughout.
2. Practice the movement in a Front Layout position with their feet in an inner tube or other flotation device. Use the cues "rotate out," "sweep out," "rotate in," and "sweep in." The swimmers should concentrate totally on the movement of their hands.
3. Practice in the proper position, with the cues "sweep" and "rotate."
4. Speed up the motion as they learn it.

Common Errors

- Rather than an equally strong inward and outward sweep, the inward movement becomes only a resting (recovery) movement. This is finning, not sculling.
- Fingers separate.
- Stiff, rigid wrists and elbows.
- Movement initiated primarily from the shoulders.
- Feet and hips sinking.

- Failure to maintain wrist hyperextension, especially on the inward sweep.

- Failure to extend ankles and toes.
- Sweeping the hands too far from the body.
- Allowing the hands to break the surface.
- Failure to lead with the wrists.

Corrections

- Use the cue words "sweep" and "rotate."

- Close fingers.
- Relax; lead with wrists; "Smooth sand."
- Initiate movement from the elbows as much as possible.
- Don't arch the upper back. Drop the arms lower in the water. Learn the movement with the face in the water.
- Make the lower arms and hands feel like windshield wipers. Keep the palms facing away from the head. Point fingertips upward.
- Extend ankles and point toes.
- Don't sweep outward more than about 12 inches.
- Scull deeper!
- Always remember to rotate the wrist and the fingertips will be in the correct position to lead.

Vertical Tuck Position

Method of Execution

The Vertical Tuck position is one of the basic body positions. To get into the position, the swimmer must first get into a Back Tuck. She begins in a Back Layout and brings her knees up, pressing them to her chest. The ankles and toes should remain extended throughout this movement. She achieves the compact Tuck position by pressing her heels to her buttocks and moving her head forward against her knees. Her back should be rounded and her knees together.

As soon as she obtains the Tuck position, the swimmer executes a partial Back Tuck Somersault, stopping when the shins are perpendicular to the surface. Swimmers should learn to perform the rotation by moving their hands toward the head with the palms facing the surface. Then, with straight arms, the swimmers should pull toward their hips. This movement will rotate the body in the direction opposite the arm movement. When the hands reach the hips, the swimmer "catches" the water and sculls with her palms facing the pool bottom. At this point, the shoulders and the back of the head are facing the bottom of the pool.

As swimmers become more advanced, they can learn a more difficult method of rotation. Performing a strong Snail scull (flexed wrists) behind the hips with the palms pointed toward the bottom of the pool, and lifting the hips while pressing the body backward, will enable the body's momentum and buoyancy to rotate the body. When the swimmer's shins are perpendicular to the water, she slides her hands forward with her fingers leading and keeps her elbows close to her body.

When the swimmer is in the Vertical Tuck position, she brings her hands just beneath the surface, close to her shins and in line with her forearms. With her elbows bent and held close to her body, she performs a sculling motion with her palms facing the bottom of the pool. The sculling motion is parallel to the surface. The little fingers should touch the lower legs as the hands sweep in during the scull.

Teaching Progression

On the Deck Have the Swimmers:

1. Assume a Tuck position and wrap their arms around their legs and squeeze. They should concentrate on making a good tuck by (a) keeping their knees together, (b) pressing their feet toward

the buttocks and their knees to the chest, (c) and moving their head forward with their nose between their knees.

2. Perform the Tuck as above without using their arms.

In the Water Have the Swimmers:

1. Assume a Back Layout position while holding onto the pool gutter with their legs extended toward the center of the pool. Have a partner assist each swimmer as the swimmer pulls her body into a Tuck and backward into the side of the pool. She should finish in a compact Tuck position with her shins vertical and pressed against the side of the pool.

2. Work away from the side with a partner. The helper helps the swimmer rotate and hold the proper position once she is in the Tuck.

3. Practice the position on their own.

Common Errors / Corrections

(See "Common Errors and Corrections" for the Somersault, Back Tuck, page 28.)

Common Errors	Corrections
• Loose tuck.	• Press heels to buttocks, knees to chest, head to knees.
• Failure to roll into a true vertical position.	• Practice against the side of the pool or with a partner until the feel of the true vertical position is obtained. The swimmer usually feels as if she has rolled too far when she is actually in the true vertical position.
• Loss of balance, causing the body to roll over.	• Check the position of the hands during the sculling motion. Unnecessary muscle tension also makes balance difficult.

Inverted Split Position With Support Scull

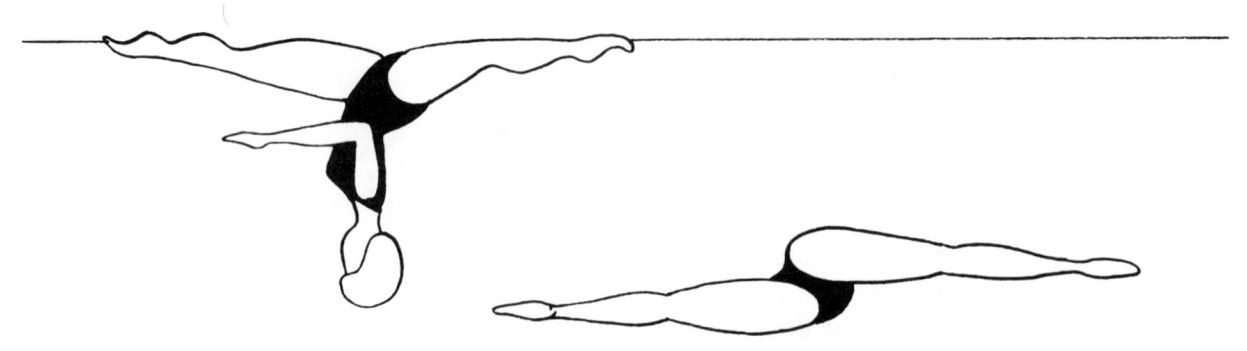

Overhead View of Inverted Split Position

Method of Execution

This figure is a combination of two separate skills—the Inverted Split position and the Support scull.

Inverted Split Position

The method that is used to obtain the Split position is open to the swimmers. However, probably the easiest method is to perform a partial Back Tuck Somersault into the Vertical Tuck position. When in the Vertical Tuck, the swimmer slowly extends one leg straight in front of her and the other leg straight behind to form a "split" position.

The feet and hips should remain as close to the surface as possible without extending out of the water. The hips must be in line with one another and directly under the mid-point of the split. The swimmer must not allow the knees to point to the sides. The back knee should point directly toward the ceiling, and the front knee should point directly toward the bottom of the pool. The swimmer must arch her lower back to keep the body in a vertical position with the shoulders under the hips. The head should be in a vertical position under the shoulders.

Support Scull

The Support scull is a stationary scull used when the body is in an inverted position. This scull makes it possible to lift the legs out of the water and hold the inverted position —which is an extremely important synchronized swimming skill.

Once in an inverted position, the swimmer performs a Support scull with her forearms and hands at waist level and perpendicular to her body. With flat hands, she lifts the little fingers and drops the thumbs to turn the palms out. She sweeps her hands about 12 inches away from her body with the thumbs leading and her elbows bent. This outward rotation is relatively difficult and creates a strain on the forearms. Most swimmers will have trouble rotating their palms outward. Even the strongest attempt may only produce a small tilt of the hands, so the palms will remain almost facing the bottom of the pool.

As soon as the swimmer reaches the end of the sweep, she rotates her hands by lifting her thumbs and dropping her little fingers. This rotation should only be a slight tilt; the hands shouldn't be rotated so far that they face one another. Rotating the hands inward is as easy as rotating the hands out is hard, so the swimmer must concentrate on keeping her palms almost facing the bottom of the pool. From this position the swimmer sweeps her hands back in with the little fingers leading. As soon as the hands are almost touching, the procedure begins again. As with other sculls, the movement of the hands should resemble a figure eight.

To maintain maximum pressure against the water, the swimmer should keep the fingers and thumb close together. Her elbows should stay fairly close to her body, and her shoulders should stay down and relaxed.

Teaching Progression

On the Deck Have the Swimmers:

1. Sit at a table. They should place both hands beneath the table top with their palms facing the bottom of the table and the hands almost touching. Direct them to sweep their hands outward about 12 inches while rotating their hands so that the little fingers stay in contact with the table and the thumbs press toward the floor. Without stopping, they should then rotate their hands so that the thumbs are in contact with the table and the little fingers are angled down slightly. The swimmers are then to sweep their hands back toward each other until they almost touch (always leading with the fingertips). Have the swimmers continue this alternating rotating and sweeping action (see figure below).

2. Lie on their backs and support themselves on their shoulders and upper arms while lifting their hips. They should get their hips into a vertical line with their shoulders. From this position, the swimmers should extend one leg forward and one leg backward. The split should be even. One knee should point straight up and the other straight down.

In the Water Have the Swimmers:

1. Assume a Front Layout position with their feet supported in a flotation device so that they can concentrate on their hands. They should perform the Support scull with their elbows by their sides and their palms facing toward the head. The scull will move them foot-first.

2. Stand on the bottom of the pool in deep water and perform the Support scull. If swimmers can remain on the bottom without floating up, they are performing the scull correctly.

3. Assume a Vertical position (see p. 15) with their backs against the side of the pool and their knees hooked over the side. Swimmers should then practice the Support scull, trying to keep the body in

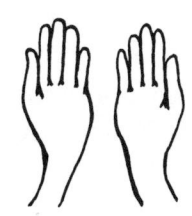

Hand position under the table

the Vertical position by the force of the scull, not by using the legs.

4. Get into an Inverted Split position by using the pool gutter to support their back foot and then extending their other foot in front to perform the split. Have partners help the swimmers achieve an even split. The same procedure can be used with the front foot on the pool gutter.

5. Assume a Split position in medium-deep water with their legs pressed against the bottom of the pool and their heads up. Swimmers should perform the Support scull in this position. If they can keep their legs against the bottom of the pool, they are sculling correctly.

6. Assume an Inverted Split position in deep water and perform the Support scull.

Common Errors

- Rather than an equally strong inward and outward sweep, the inward movement becomes only a resting (recovery) movement. This is finning, not sculling.

- Pressing the hands toward the bottom of the pool in an up-and-down movement rather than a scull.

- Allowing the pressure of the water to turn the palms so that they face each other on the inward sweep of the scull.

- Allowing the elbows to move too far away from the body during the sculling action.

- Using too large a sweep in the sculling action.

- Uneven split with one leg extending out of the water.

- Body not centered directly under the mid-line of the split.

- Hips low in the water and/or not aligned with each other. Knees not straight up and down.

Corrections

- Use the cue words "sweep" and "rotate."

- Maintain the correct sculling action.

- Hands must be tilted only slightly, and the palms should face the bottom of the pool.

- Keep the elbows close to the sides.

- The sweep should be only about 12 inches.

- Have a partner help the swimmer get the feel of a correct split.

- If the body is under the front leg, push forward with the hips, and back with the shoulders. Move the chest away from the thigh and look for the bottom of the pool.

  If the body is under the back leg, tuck the chin, pull the head forward, and straighten the back to reduce the arch.

- Perform flexibility exercises to be able to do the splits.

Ballet Leg, Single and Alternate

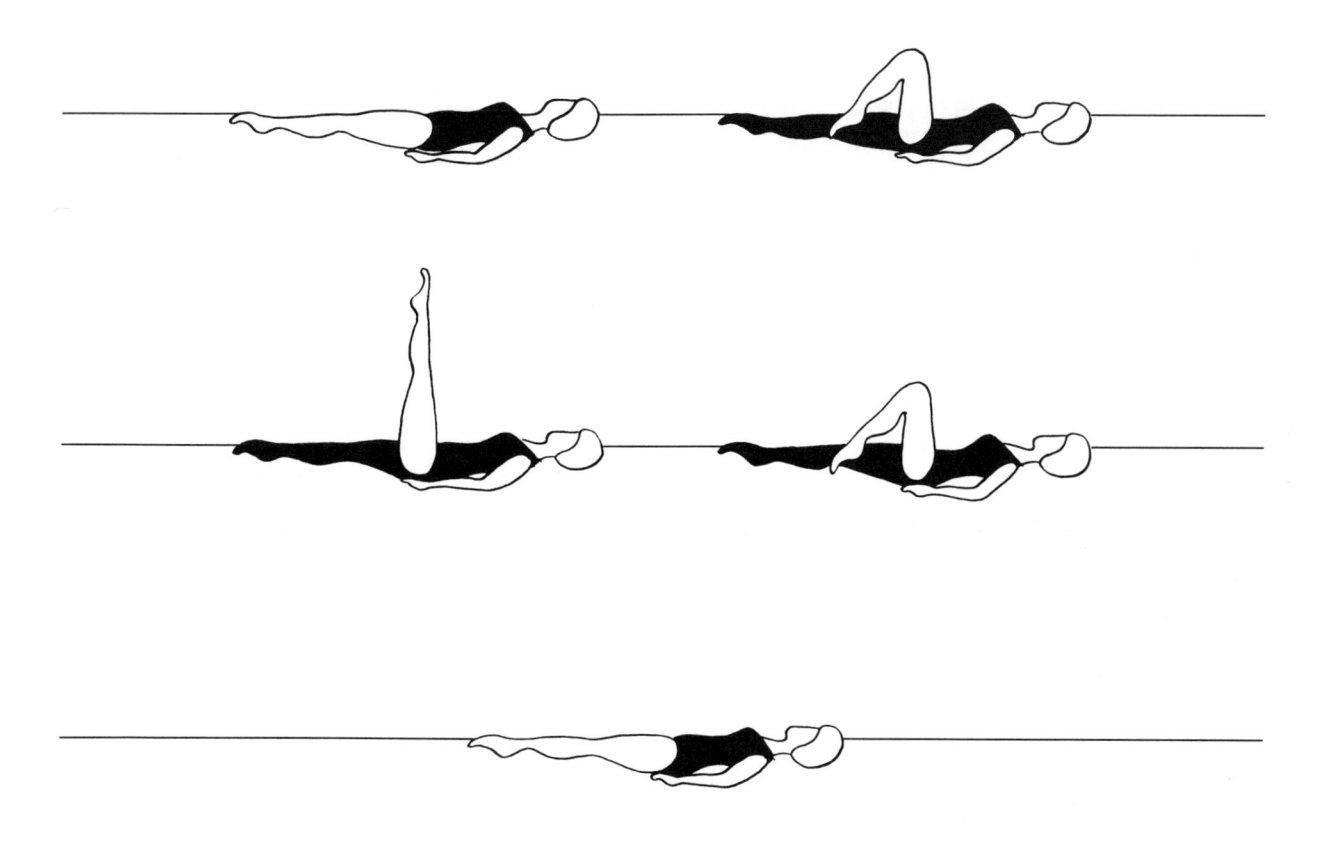

Method of Execution

To perform a Single Ballet Leg, the swimmer starts in a Back Layout position. While using a stationary Eel scull, she draws one leg up the inside of the other leg until it is in a Bent Knee position. The thigh will be perpendicular to the surface. From this position, the swimmer lifts the bent leg until it is fully extended in a vertical position from the hip. The swimmer should keep the thigh absolutely still while drawing the lower leg up. The movement from the bent knee to the fully extended position should be slow, controlled, and continuous.

The swimmer returns to the Back Layout position by reversing the procedure. First she flexes at the knee and returns the lower leg to the Bent Knee position. Once again, the movement is entirely in the lower leg and the thigh must remain still. From the Bent Knee position, the swimmer slides the foot back along the extended leg and returns it to the horizontal position, finishing in the Back Layout. The lowering of the leg should be a slow, controlled, continuous movement.

To perform an Alternate Ballet Leg the swimmer starts with a Single Ballet Leg. As soon as she finishes the Single Ballet Leg, the swimmer performs the same figure with the formerly horizontal leg. There should not be a pause between the two figures.

Teaching Progression

On the Deck Have the Swimmers:

1. Assume a Back Layout position and lift their feet, head, and hands two inches off the deck to simulate the slightly piked position in the water. In this position, they should perform the Ballet Leg first with one leg, then with the other, and then lower their feet, head, and hands to the deck. Swimmers should concentrate on moving from one position to the next with proper form in a slow, continuous, controlled movement.

In the Water Have the Swimmers:

1. Practice the Ballet Leg while supporting their horizontal leg on the pool gutter.
2. Practice the Ballet Leg while a partner supports the heel of the horizontal leg.
3. Support their horizontal leg with a flotation device while practicing the Ballet Leg.
4. Practice the Ballet Leg without support.

Common Errors / Corrections

(See "Common Errors and Corrections" for the Bent Knee Position, Scull, Supine, p. 61.)

Common Errors	Corrections
• The knee moves toward the chest while the leg is lifted.	• "Lock" the thigh in place and lift the leg from the knee up to the toes.
• The knee is bent when the leg is in the extended vertical position.	• Perform flexibility exercises to stretch the hamstring muscles (back of thigh). Sitting toe touches are one example.
• The vertical leg is over the trunk rather than being in a true vertical position over the hip.	• Push back on the knee, heel, head, and shoulders to open up the pike at the hips.
• The hips start to pike as the leg is lifted.	• Push back on the head and shoulders. Lift the heel of the horizontal leg.
• Failure to keep the foot of the horizontal leg at the surface and/or bending the knee.	• Lift the heel and lock the knee. Squeeze the buttock muscles together.
• Lowering the chin to watch the leg.	• Keep the head in line with the body. The ears should be underwater, the neck extended, and the shoulders down and relaxed. The eyes should be focused on the ceiling.

Walkover, Front

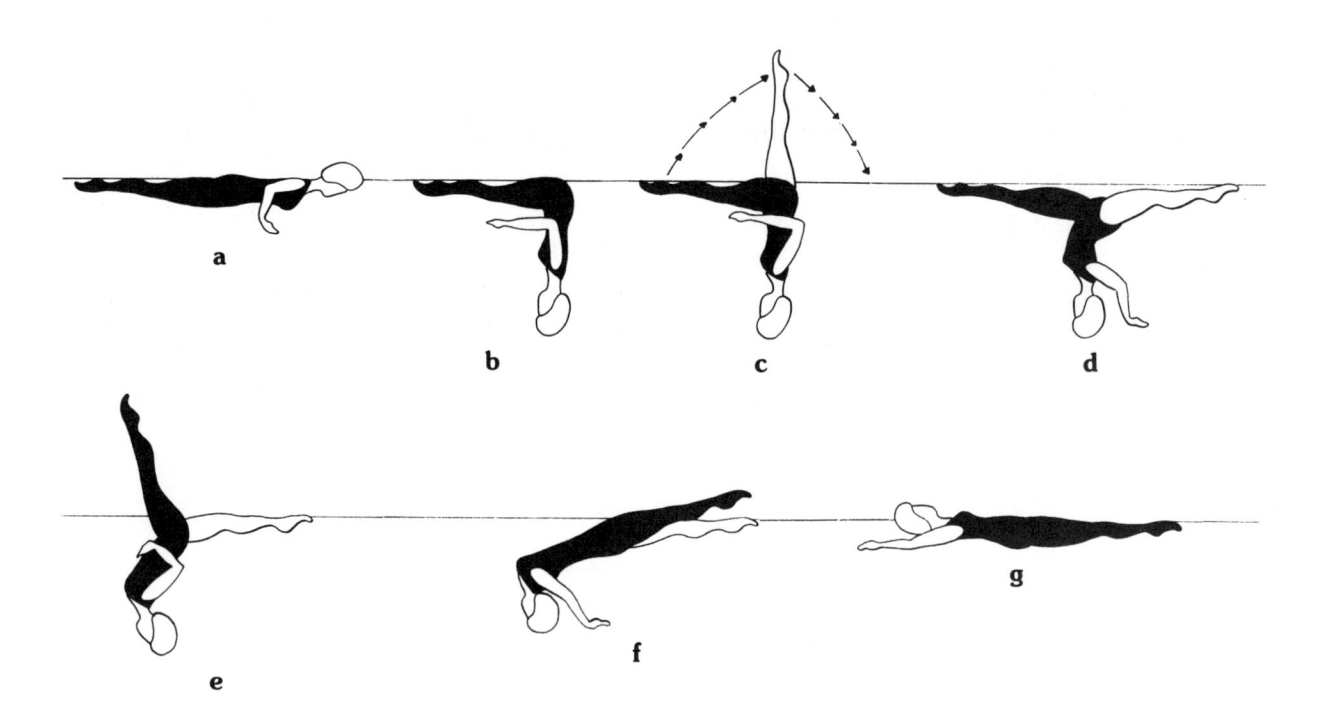

Method of Execution

The swimmer begins the Front Walkover just like the Front Pike Somersault. She first assumes a Front Layout position, then pulls down into a Front Pike. As the body reaches the 90-degree angle of the Front Pike, she lifts one leg and keeps it extended while she moves it in an arc over the water. To move the leg, the swimmer can press her hands toward the bottom of the pool, keeping her palms flat. Other arm movements are also acceptable. The hips should remain in a relatively stationary position during the arc. When the leg completes the arc, the swimmer will be in the Inverted Split position. She holds this position exactly as described on page 80.

After holding the position momentarily, the swimmer lifts the leg extended in front to meet the leg extended behind. She can perform the lift by returning her hands to a position beside her knees with her palms facing the pool bottom (see Figures c-e) and pressing down and backward to a position behind her head (see Figures e, f).

As the second leg passes the vertical point, the trunk should be in a maximum arched position. As the leg completes the arc and joins the first leg, the hands should be in a position over the head, and the swimmer should perform a Reverse Torpedo scull to prevent the body from moving foot-first too much. The swimmer controls the ascent of the body by continuing the scull until the head surfaces and the body obtains a Back Layout position. The body should travel only enough so that the head finishes in the position in which the hips started.

Teaching Progression

In the Water Have the Swimmers:

1. Get into a Split position facing away from the side of the pool and supporting the back leg on the pool gutter. Have them lift the front leg in an arc to join the leg resting on the gutter.

2. Get into a Split position facing the side of the pool and supporting the front leg on the pool gutter. Have them lift the leg resting on the gutter in an arc to join the other leg and perform the Reverse Torpedo scull to obtain the Back Layout position.

3. Get into a Front Pike position facing the side of the pool with their feet resting on the gutter. Then have them practice the Front Walkover from this position.

4. Assume a Front Pike position in waist-deep water, with their hands on the bottom of the pool. From this position, they can perform a Walkover by moving the legs through the Walkover motions and then unrolling the body into the Back Layout position.

5. Perform the entire movement in deep water.

Common Errors / Corrections

(See "Common Errors and Corrections" for the Somersault, Front Pike, page 51, and the Inverted Split Position with Support Scull, page 82.)

- Lifting the second leg over before the first leg reaches the surface in a Split position.
  - Press down with the second leg until the first leg touches the water in the Split position.

- Splashing when lifting and lowering the legs.
  - The leg must be on the surface at the beginning of the lift. Tighten the leg muscles and exert control when lowering the legs. The second leg is especially prone to splash during its movement. Keep the head down and the lower back in an extreme arch.

- Feet sinking after they meet.
  - Press up on the toes. Maintain the back arch.

- Extreme foot-first movement at the end of the figure.
  - Control movement with the Reverse Torpedo scull, with the hands behind the head.

Dolphin, Bent Knee

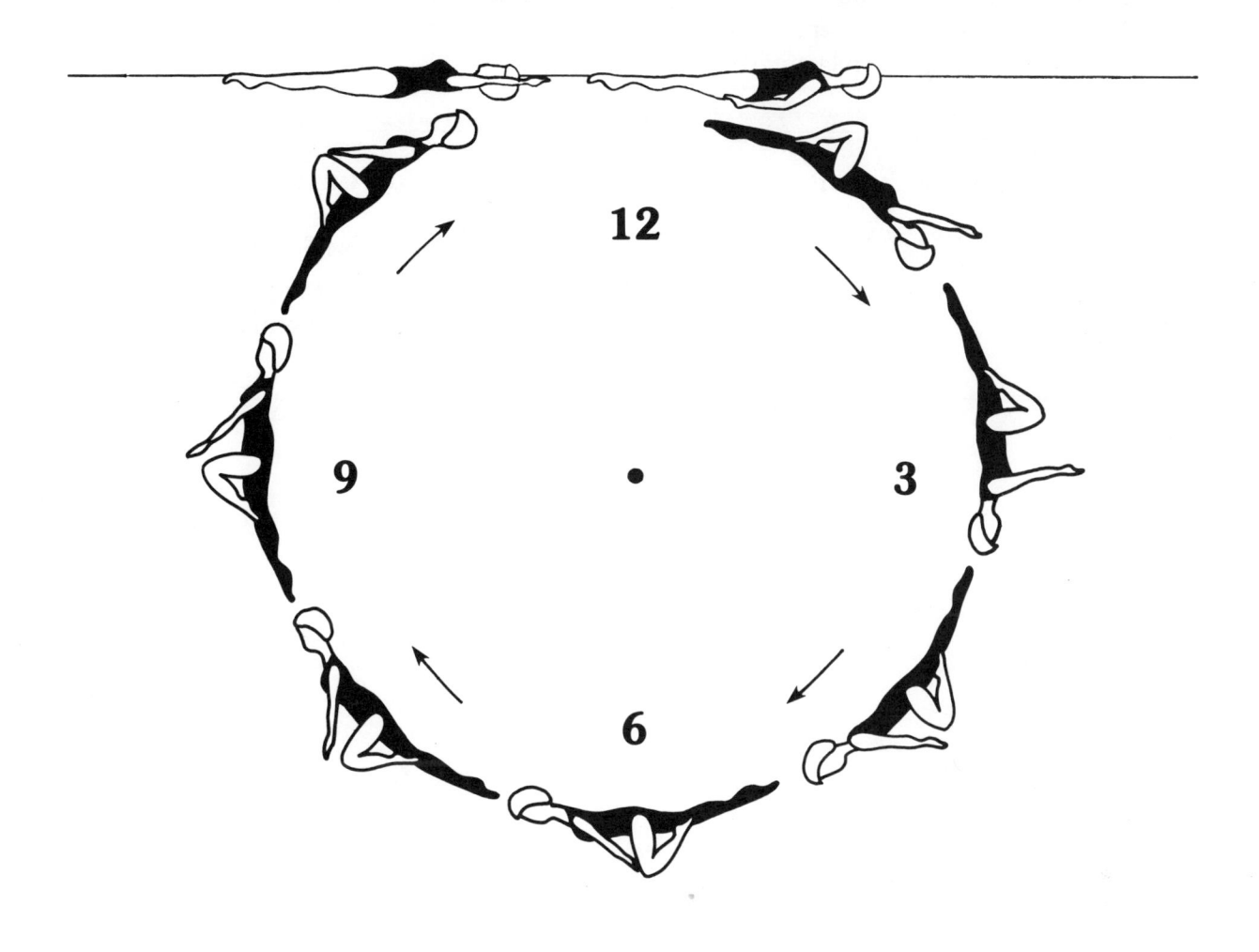

Method of Execution

The Bent Knee Dolphin is executed almost exactly like the Head-First Dolphin explained on pages 69-71. The swimmer starts in a Back Layout position and uses her arms to begin the movement to submerge. Just before her knees begin to submerge, the swimmer brings one knee to the Bent Knee position, drawing the foot along the inside of the other leg until it is at or above the knee. The swimmer should be in the Bent Knee position before the foot of the extended leg submerges.

The swimmer continues the Dolphin in the Bent Knee position. When the bent knee breaks the surface as the body is returning to the surface, the swimmer straightens the knee by sliding it along the inside of the opposite leg. This movement returns the body to a Back Layout position. As the hips surface, the swimmer should use a strong Eel scull to help support the body and control the movement of the leg as it straightens. Refer to the Head-First Dolphin for complete information on the position of the arms and the rest of the body during this figure.

Teaching Progression

Use the same teaching progression as for the Head-First Dolphin, except have the swimmers bend one knee while entering the water and straighten it during the return to the Back Layout.

Common Errors	Corrections
(See "Common Errors and Corrections" for the Dolphin, Head-First, page 70.)	
• Improper Bent Knee position.	• The foot of the bent leg should be at or above the knee on the inside of the opposite leg.

Porpoise

Method of Execution

To perform the Porpoise the swimmer first assumes a Front Layout position. She then pulls down into a Front Pike position with the buttocks, legs, and feet traveling along the surface. Once in the Front Pike, the swimmer lifts both legs to a Vertical position in line with her trunk. The swimmer lifts her legs by squeezing the buttock muscles. She can provide additional lift for the legs by placing her hands just under her knees with the palms facing down and pressing diagonally back and down toward her shoulders.

As swimmers become more skilled and stronger, they can use a Support scull while they lift their legs.

The swimmer holds the vertical position for a moment, and then descends. If the swimmer pressed with her hands toward her shoulders to perform the leg lift, in order to hold the vertical position she should press straight down until her arms are extended over her head. The swimmer controls the rate of descent with her scull. Once the swimmer is more skilled, she can use a Support scull to hold the vertical position. The figure is finished when swimmer's toes submerge.

Teaching Progression

On the Deck Have the Swimmers:

1. Lie on the deck and assume a 6 o'clock Pike position (see p. 51) with the backs of their hands against their knees. From this position, they should press their arms up and sideways to shoulder level and simultaneously lower their legs to a horizontal position. The legs should remain horizontal, while the arms continue to an extended position over the head.

In the Water Have the Swimmers:

1. Assume a Front Pike position with their backs against the side of the pool. While holding onto the gutter, the swimmers are to lift their legs to the Vertical position.

2. Assume a Front Pike position in the water with their backs against the side of the pool. Rather than holding onto the gutter, each swimmer should have a partner press her against the side. The swimmer is to place the back of her hands under her knees with the palms facing toward the bottom of the pool. She should then lift her legs while pressing down with her hands. At the conclusion of the press, her thumbs should touch the pool wall at shoulder level.

3. Get into a Front Layout position with their feet hooked over the pool gutter. From this position they should perform the Front Pike pull-down and the arm press and leg lift.

4. Practice the entire figure in deep water.

Common Errors

- Overpiking the body before the leg lift.

- Piking from the waist instead of at the hips.

- Lifting the legs too far which results in arching or leaning onto the back in the vertical position.

Corrections

- The body usually feels underpiked when it is actually at the 90-degree Pike position. The leg lift should begin just before the body reaches a 90-degree angle.

- Lead with the chest in the pull-down and arch the lower back even though the body is piking.

- It usually feels as if the legs have not been lifted enough when they are in the Vertical position. Keep the head in line with the shoulders. Look at the pool wall, not the bottom of the pool.

SEQUENCE 4

"Fiddler on the Roof" by Jerry Bock

The swimmer must choreograph her own routine for this unit. She must use at least 28 measures of the music and include all of the skills listed below. The skills do not have to appear in the order they are listed. She should use skills from Units I-III as well.

In the sequence the swimmer should proceed in a logical pattern and use as much of the pool as possible. How the swimmer connects the skills and what she selects from previous units should accentuate her best points and suit her capabilities. Each movement should be precise and controlled, and the swimmer should exhibit style and confidence.

To choreograph the piece, the swimmer should tape the music, listen to it several times, and draw up a chart like those used in the previous units. She should imagine herself doing various moves while listening to the music and then write them down on her chart. Once the swimmer has several measures choreographed, she should try the sequence on dry land and then in the water to see if it flows and allows her time to move from figure to figure. The swimmer should then alter sections which don't work and try out the modified sequence. This process should continue until the swimmer has choreographed at least 28 measures.

The swimmer should use the same method described in previous units to memorize her routine.

Required Skills for Unit IV Sequence

Note: These skills do not have to appear in the following order.

- Ballet Leg (Right Leg)
- Ballet Leg (Left Leg)
- Walkover, Front
- Dolphin, Bent Knee
- Porpoise
- Eggbeater with one arm out of the water (using creative arm strokes)
- Eggbeater with both arms out of the water (using creative arm strokes)
- A creative figure using the Vertical Tuck position
- At least one figure from Unit III

UNIT V

Unit V Skill Performance Objectives

Swimmers should be able to perform the following skills for the designated distances or in the designated ways.

Strokes and Transitions:

Eggbeater Kick, Traveling—15 yards

Basic Positions and Sculls:

Flamingo Position

Crane Position

Figures:

Ballet Leg Submarine, Single

Somersub

Walkover, Back

Barracuda

Sequence:

Performed to "Yellow Rose of Texas" adapted by Don George

Eggbeater Kick, Traveling

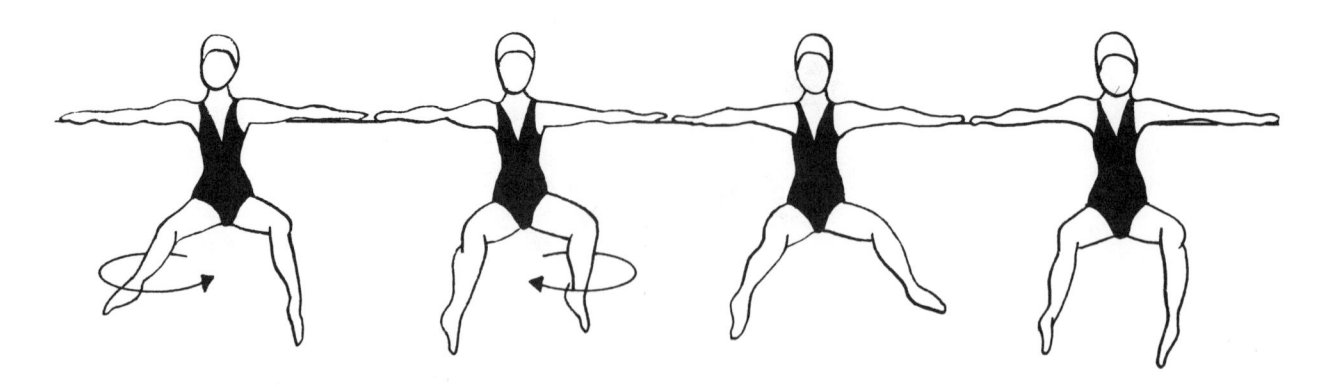

Method of Execution

Basically, the Traveling Eggbeater is performed exactly the same as the Stationary Eggbeater (see pp. 74-75). However, in order to travel the swimmer needs to make a few adjustments in body position. If the swimmer wants to *move forward*, she must lower her knees and make about a 90-degree angle between her lower and upper legs. In this position she pushes the water behind her with her feet. If the swimmer wants to *move backward*, she lifts her knees and keeps her feet in front of her body. She then kicks the water in front of her. Swimmers usually find moving backward the easiest direction to travel.

To *move to either side*, the swimmer puts the leg on the lead side beneath her body and her other leg to the other side. She will feel as if she is leaning in the direction in which she is traveling. For example, if she wants to move to the right, the right leg should be directly beneath her body and the left leg pushes the water as it trails on the left side of her body. If the swimmer wants to move to the left, she reverses the procedure.

Teaching Progression

To review the Eggbeater kick, the swimmer should go through the steps described on page 74.

In the Water Have the Swimmers:

1. Practice traveling by moving around in a square while using just the Eggbeater kick. They can use the lines on the pool bottom to make sure they are traveling in straight lines. Make sure they go in both directions around the square.

Common Errors

Corrections

(See "Common Errors and Corrections" for the Eggbeater Kick, p. 75.)

- Lack of speed and height.
- Using the hands to get or stay higher.

- Practice, practice, practice. It will come.
- Use the legs only.

Flamingo Position

Method of Execution

To perform the Flamingo the swimmer first assumes a Single Ballet Leg position. She must keep the muscles in the vertical leg tight in order to keep it in position during the rest of the movement. To go into the Flamingo the swimmer draws the horizontal leg toward her chest until the middle of the calf is at the knee of the vertical leg. The thigh should not touch the chest. The shin stays at the surface and the foot is extended.

While drawing the leg back, the swimmer prevents her back from rounding by lifting her chest and pressing her shoulders back. The shoulders should stay down and relaxed. The back of the head and neck should be pressed into the water.

Teaching Progression

On the Deck Have the Swimmers:

1. Practice the Flamingo position while lying on the deck. They should concentrate on keeping the horizontal leg parallel to the deck as they draw it toward the chest. They can use their arms to help support their body.

In the Water Have the Swimmers:

1. Practice the Flamingo position with the foot of the horizontal leg on the pool gutter.
2. Get into the Flamingo position and have a partner help support the horizontal leg.
3. Practice the Flamingo position without support.
4. Move forward and backward in the Flamingo position by using the Eel and Snail sculls.

Common Errors

- Knees are together instead of the mid-calf of the horizontal leg being against the knee of the vertical leg.
- Falling backward.

Corrections

- Pull the bent knee toward the chest and press back on the vertical knee.

- Sit lower in the water until the sculling action is stronger.

Common Errors (cont.)

- Falling forward.

- Sculling at waist level.

- Sinking beneath the surface.

- Toes and/or foot of the horizontal leg are beneath the surface.

- Body is collapsed; chest is low in the water.

Corrections (cont.)

- Push the shoulders and head back. Press the extended leg away from the face.

- Scull at hip level to support the heaviest part of the body.

- Continue to scull while holding the Flamingo position. The body will slowly resurface. Check for correct sculling action.

- Press the heel and toes up.

- Push the shoulders and head back against the water. Open the Pike position.

Crane Position

Method of Execution

The method the swimmer uses to get into a Crane position is open to the swimmer. The following three methods are the most common:

1. From a Front Pike pull-down, the swimmer lifts one leg to a vertical position.

2. The swimmer gets into a Vertical position

underwater and lowers one leg as the body rises to a controllable height.

3. The swimmer performs a partial Back Tuck Somersault to a Vertical Tuck position and extends one leg horizontally in front of her and one leg vertically.

In the Crane position, the horizontal leg must be at a right angle to the vertical leg and the body. It should also be parallel to the surface. The swimmer should be able to hold this position without traveling by performing a Support scull under the horizontal leg. Although swimmers will want to have the vertical leg as far out of the water as possible, it is best for them to learn the skill with the water at knee level or lower if necessary.

Teaching Progression

On the Deck Have the Swimmers:
1. Stand against a wall with their backs flat and their hips tucked under. Their shoulders should be down and relaxed. The chin should be tucked in and the neck pressed against the wall. Have partners help the swimmers extend one leg horizontally so that it is parallel to the deck.

In the Water Have the Swimmers:
1. Assume an inverted position with their backs flat against the side of the pool. They should hook one knee over the side and lower the other leg to a horizontal position in the water while performing a Support scull.

2. Start in an inverted position with their backs against the side of the pool. Have partners help the swimmers remain against the wall while they assume a Crane position by leaving one leg vertical and bringing the other to the horizontal position. During this movement the swimmers should be performing a Support scull.

3. Practice the entire technique. Allow them to try different methods of getting into the Crane position.

Common Errors

- Failure to maintain a right angle between the legs.

- Overextension of the vertical leg so that it is arched toward the back.

- Tipping forward toward the horizontal leg.

Corrections

- Press down on the horizontal leg so that it is at a right angle to the trunk and parallel to the surface.

- Move the leg toward the face.

- This problem may be caused by a slightly piked position or by sculling too far in front of the body.

Ballet Leg Submarine, Single

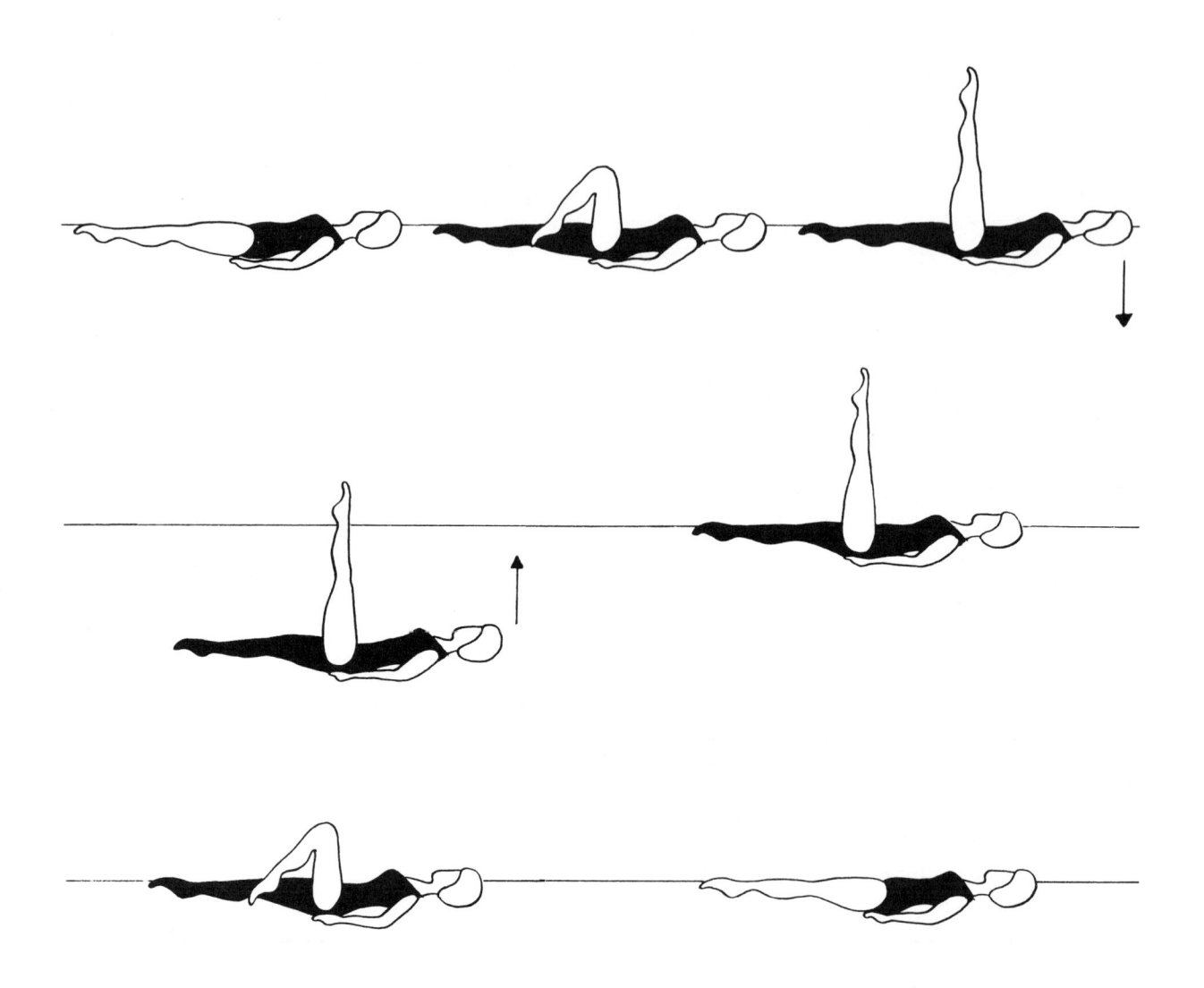

Method of Execution

The swimmer starts by assuming a Ballet Leg position from a Back Layout. While remaining in the Ballet Leg position, she submerges her body so that the water line on the extended leg is between the knee and the ankle. The swimmer can make her body submerge by sculling at her hips with the palms facing the surface and exerting upward pressure. Another method she can use to submerge, is to have her palms face the surface and move her hands slightly higher in the water than her head while exerting upward pressure. As the body descends, the swimmer needs to lift her hips so that the body will remain perfectly straight and extended. She remains submerged by exerting upward pressure while sculling with her hands either at her hips or above her head.

If the swimmer submerged by sculling with her hands at her hips, to return the body to the surface she turns her palms over to face the bottom of the pool and executes a flat

Eel scull. If the swimmer was sculling with her hands above her head, she turns the hands sideways with the little fingers leading and slices the hands to the hips before turning her palms over and performing the flat Eel scull. Once the body is at the surface again, she lowers the vertical leg and resumes the Back Layout position. The swimmer should remain stationary during the figure. She shouldn't move forward or backward.

Teaching Progression

On the Deck Have the Swimmers:
1. Lie in a Ballet Leg position and try both of the sculling positions that can be used to submerge the body.

In the Water Have the Swimmers:
1. Lie on the bottom of the shallow end of the pool in a Ballet Leg position. The swimmers may need a partner to help them stay on the bottom and not float toward the surface. From the bottom they should scull to the surface in the Ballet Leg position.

2. Practice the entire figure.

Common Errors

- The horizontal leg floats up as the body submerges.

- The head moves forward and the shoulders round.
- The body moves head first as it rises to the surface.
- The vertical leg moves toward the face as the body submerges.

Corrections

- Maintain full body extension and press down on the heel. In the submerged position, when the horizontal leg is in line with the body and parallel to the surface, the swimmer will feel as though the leg is much lower than the head.
- Keep the head in line with the body and press the shoulders back.
- Flex the wrists so that the fingertips point down slightly.
- Press the shoulders back and the vertical leg away from the face as the body descends.

Somersub

Method of Execution

This figure is a combination of the Front Pike Somersault and the Single Ballet Leg Submarine. The swimmer begins by assuming a Front Layout position, extends her arms over her head and performs a pulldown into a Front Pike. Just as in the Front Pike Somersault, as the swimmer's trunk moves down to assume the Front Pike position, the buttocks, legs and feet move along the surface and the hips should reach the point at which the head started. The swimmer should exert light upward tension on the muscles in front of the legs and press up on the heels to help keep the hips and heels at the surface.

The swimmer locks the body in the 90-degree Front Pike position and continues the Somersault until the trunk is parallel to the surface and the legs are perpendicular to the surface, as in a 6 o'clock Front Pike position. The swimmer moves her arms in the same small circular pulls used for the Front Pike Somersault.

The swimmer then lowers one leg to a horizontal positon so that her body assumes a Single Ballet Leg Submarine. The horizontal leg must be in line with the body and parallel to the surface. The water level on the vertical leg should stay constant as the other leg is lowered. While lowering one leg to the horizontal position, the swimmer can perform one of the following: (a) an Eel scull with flat palms at her hips; (b) small circles with her arms beneath the level of her shoulders, her elbows bent and her palms facing toward her body; or (c) a stationary Torpedo scull overhead with her elbows bent.

After lowering her leg the swimmer is in the Single Ballet Leg Submarine position. To scull her body to the surface, the swimmer uses a flat Eel scull at the hips. Her head and feet should surface simultaneously. If she used an overhead scull while lowering the leg to horizontal, she needs to slice the hands back to the hips, leading with the little fingers and then proceed to use the flat Eel scull. To prevent head-first movement while surfacing, the swimmer might need to flex her wrists slightly.

Once the swimmer has surfaced, she lowers the vertical leg to the Bent Knee position and then extends it to the horizontal position. The figure finishes in this Back Layout.

Teaching Progression

Note: Have swimmers review the Front Pike Somersault and the Single Ballet Leg Submarine before working on the Somersub.

On the Deck Have the Swimmers:

1. Assume a 90-degree Pike position (6 o'clock Front Pike) while lying on their backs. Then have them proceed to lower one leg to the deck.

In the Water Have the Swimmers:

1. Lie on the bottom of the shallow end of the pool in a 6 o'clock Front Pike position. The swimmers may need a partner to help them stay on the bottom and not float toward the surface. While at the bottom they should lower one leg to a horizontal position on the pool bottom. They should then scull to the surface in the Ballet Leg position.

2. Start in a Front Layout, perform a partial Front Pike Somersault, and stop in the 6 o'clock Front Pike position with their ankles out of the water. The swimmers should practice balancing in this position.

3. Practice the entire figure.

Common Errors	Corrections
(See "Common Errors and Corrections" for the Somersault, Front Pike, p. 51, and the Ballet Leg Submarine, Single, p. 97.)	
• Failure to lower the horizontal leg so that it is parallel to the surface.	• When the horizontal leg is in line with the body and parallel to the surface, it will feel as though it is much lower than the head.
• Front Pike Somersault stops too soon. Swimmer looks like she is standing on her head slightly.	• Continue the Front Pike Somersault until the trunk is parallel to the bottom of the pool and the surface.
• Dropping the leg to a submerged Ballet Leg position and surfacing simultaneously.	• Assume the submerged Ballet Leg position completely before resurfacing.
• Dropping the vertical leg to a Bent Knee position while resurfacing.	• Completely resurface with the face out of the water. Hold the Ballet Leg position momentarily before returning to a Back Layout position.

Common Errors (cont.)

- Head surfaces before the foot of the horizontal leg.

- The foot of the horizontal leg surfaces before the head.

Corrections (cont.)

- Press back on the head and shoulders. The head and foot must surface simultaneously.

- Press down on the heel of the horizontal leg. The head and foot must surface simultaneously.

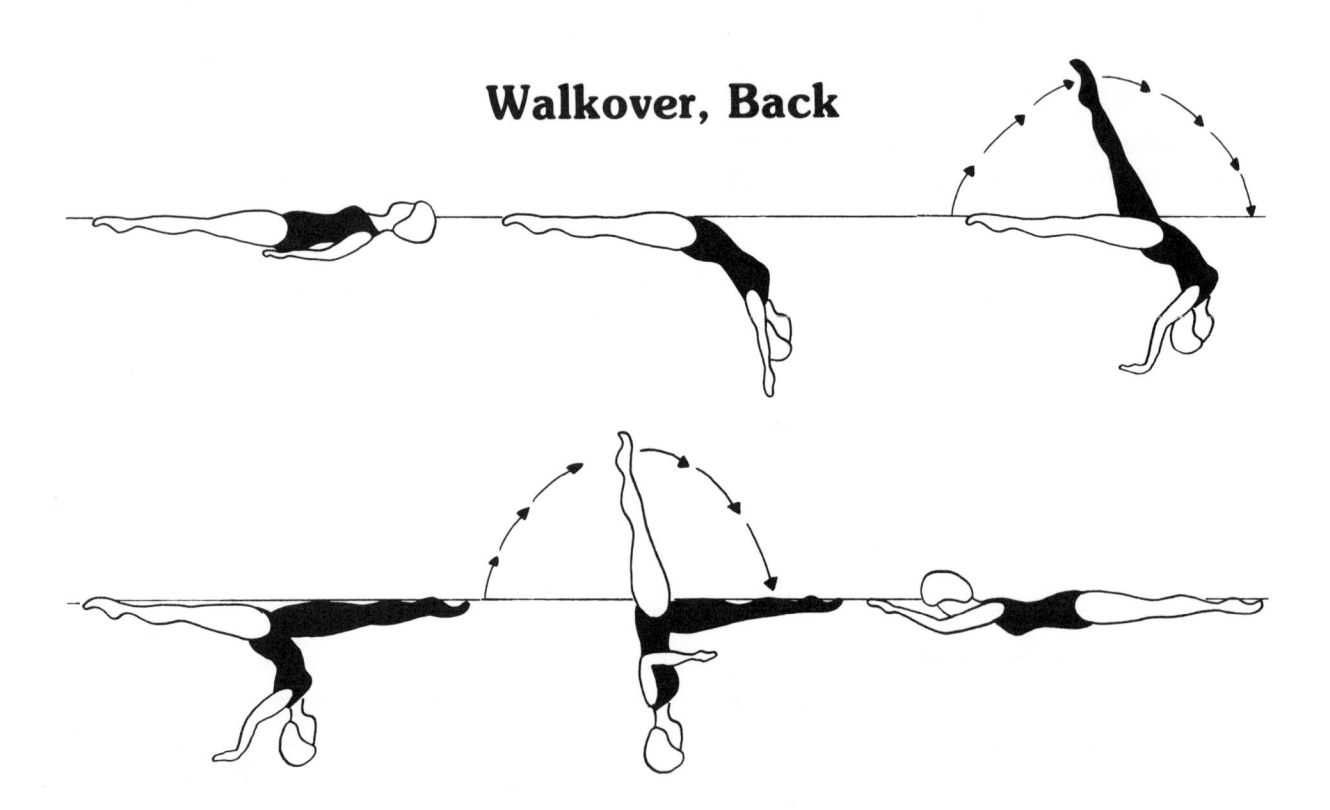

Walkover, Back

Method of Execution

To perform the Back Walkover the swimmer first assumes a Back Layout position. The swimmer begins as if she were going to perform a Head-First Dolphin, by arching her back gently, pressing her shoulders back, and pressing her heels up so that her feet stay at the surface. When her head reaches a position under her hips, the swimmer keeps her head and torso in that position. She then lifts one leg and moves it in an arc over the surface until it is horizontal in front of her in an Inverted Split position. To keep the body in position while the leg arcs, the swimmer slices her hands to her hips and then presses toward the head while moving the hands behind the body. Alternatively, the swimmer can place her hands and forearms well behind her shoulders at head level and scull.

The swimmer holds the Inverted Split position by using a stationary scull close to her head. After holding the split for a moment, the swimmer lifts the second leg in an arc to join the first leg. To accompany the leg lift, the swimmer moves her hands to a Support scull position under her forward knee, with the palms facing the bottom of the pool, and presses down and back to a position behind her head.

As the second leg passes the vertical point, the swimmer begins to move her head slightly toward the surface in order to open up the Pike position between the trunk and front leg. To prevent excessive foot-first movement, the swimmer should move her hands to a position over her head and scull with the wrists flexed. The swimmer continues to lift her trunk toward the surface as the second leg lowers to meet the other leg. The swimmer finishes in a Front Layout position. She should only move far enough so that her head finishes where her hips were when she was in the Inverted Split position.

Teaching Progression

In the Water Have the Swimmers:

1. Assume an Inverted Split position with their front foot resting on the pool gutter. They should lift the back leg in an arc to join the leg resting on the pool gutter.

2. Assume an Inverted Split position with their back foot resting on the pool gutter. They should lift the back leg in an arc to join the other leg. As they lift their back leg, the swimmers should open the Pike and scull to a Front Layout position.

3. Get into a Back Layout position with both feet resting on the pool gutter. They should start the Dolphin motion by arching away from the side of the pool and execute a Back Walkover. Swimmers may need a partner to help them keep their feet on the gutter.

4. Assume a 90-degree Front Pike position. They should then scull to return to a Front Layout position.

5. Practice the entire figure.

Common Errors   Corrections

(See the first three "Common Errors and Corrections" for Dolphin, Head-First, p. 70, and the "Common Errors and Corrections" for the Inverted Split Position, p. 82.)

- Lifting the second leg over before the first has reached the surface.

- Press down on the second leg until the first has touched the water and an Inverted Split position is achieved.

- Splashing when lifting and lowering the legs.

- The leg must be on the surface at the beginning of the lift. Tighten the leg muscles and exert control in lowering the legs. The second leg is prone to splash on lowering. This is especially likely to occur if the head is brought up too soon.

- Feet sinking after they meet.

- Don't move the head up too soon.

- Extreme foot-first movement as the swimmer moves into the Front Layout.

- Control the movement by sculling with flexed wrists.

Barracuda

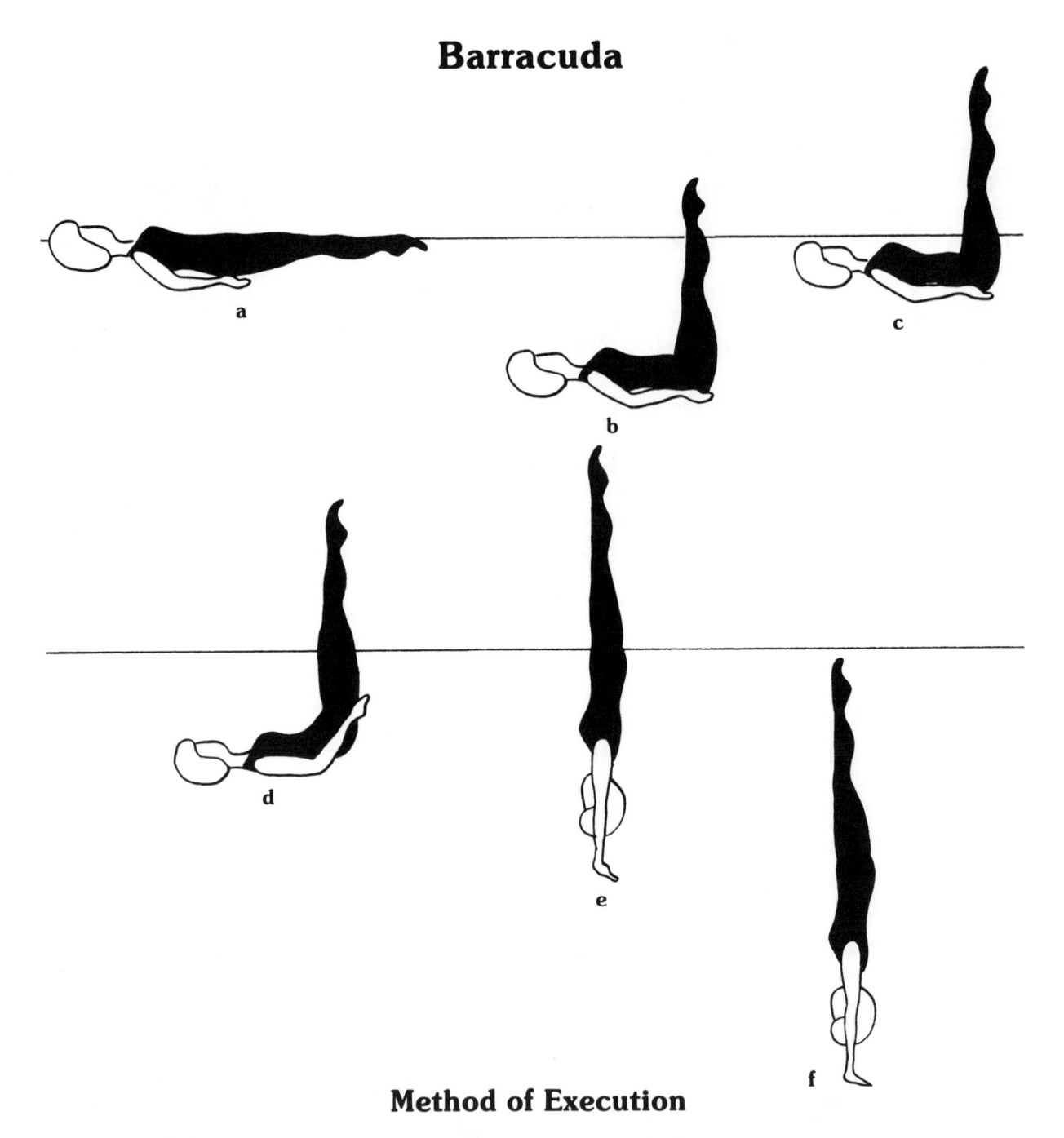

Method of Execution

The swimmer first assumes a Back Layout position. She then lifts her legs sharply so that her trunk is at a right angle to her legs. Simultaneously, she moves her arms sideways and overhead while keeping them underwater with the palms facing the surface. The body will submerge, but the ankles and feet should stay above the water. The swimmer maintains the Pike underwater by using a flat scull overhead.

The swimmer then lifts the body slightly by moving the hands sideways with the little fingers leading and slicing to the hips. It may be necessary to execute several small circles to establish balance at this point (see Figure d). By sculling as far behind the hips as possible, the swimmer lifts the hips and begins to move to the Vertical position with her body. She assumes the Vertical position by collapsing the abdomen into the small of her back and unrolling the torso one vertebra at a time from the tailbone to the neck.

When the body unrolls to the point at which the hands must turn over for support, the swimmer moves her hands from her hips with the fingertips leading and the palms facing the bottom. With a continuous motion, she turns her palms over and moves the hands inward toward the hips and then forward at waist level, all with the fingertips leading. This arm action provides support for the swimmer by putting constant pressure against the water. Throughout the arm action the swimmer continues to unroll to reach the Vertical position (see Figures d, e).

The arm action is open to the swimmers for this figure. The procedure outlined here will work for most swimmers. Experienced swimmers may use alternative methods.

The swimmer should hold the height of the Vertical position momentarily and then descend, while remaining in the Vertical position. The swimmer controls the speed of her descent by sculling overhead. The figure ends after the toes submerge, and the swimmer holds the Vertical position momentarily.

Teaching Progression

On the Deck Have the Swimmers:

1. Sit with their legs together and extended. They should collapse their abdomens into the small of their backs and unroll the torso one vertebra at a time to reach a Back Layout position.

2. Stand and pike at the hips until their trunks are parallel to the deck. The swimmers should then perform the arm action of the Barracuda and unroll the back at the appropriate time.

In the Water Have the Swimmers:

1. Hook their legs over the side with their backs facing the bottom. They should be in a 90-degree Pike position with their thighs against the side of the pool. Have the swimmers unroll the body one vertebra at a time until the trunk is in a Vertical position, in line with their thighs and against the side of the pool.

2. Start in a Back Layout position and practice piking into the submerged 6 o'clock Front Pike position. They should work on achieving proper position and balance.

3. Practice the entire figure.

Common Errors

- During the movement from the Back Layout to the submerged 6 o'clock position, the feet sink.

- Upward thrust of the legs and unrolling of the body are executed as the hands slice from overhead to the hips.

- Attempting to move into a Vertical position by pushing the shoulders back instead of unrolling.

- Attempting to move into a Vertical position by pushing the hips back over the head instead of unrolling the body under the hips.

Corrections

- Move the hands overhead sooner.

- Move the hands to the hips and stabilize the position before starting the upward thrust of the legs and unrolling the body.

- Collapse the abdomen into the small of the back and unroll one vertebra at a time from the tailbone to the neck.

- Unroll the body instead of pushing the shoulders back.

SEQUENCE 5

"Yellow Rose of Texas" adapted by Don George

The swimmer must choreograph her own routine for this unit. She must use at least 32 measures of the music and include all of the skills listed below. The skills do not have to appear in the order in which they are listed. The swimmer should use skills from Units I-IV as well.

Just as with the sequence she created for Unit IV, the swimmer should proceed in a logical pattern and use as much of the pool as possible. How the swimmer combines the skills and what she selects from previous units should accentuate her best points and suit her capabilities. Each movement should be precise and controlled, and the swimmer should exhibit style and confidence.

The swimmer should use the same method for choreographing and learning the piece as discussed in Unit IV, page 90.

Required Skills for Unit V Sequence

Note: These skills do not have to appear in the following order.

- Flamingo Position
- Ballet Leg Submarine, Single
- Walkover, Back
- Barracuda
- Eggbeater moving sideways with creative arm strokes
- A creative figure using a Crane Position
- At least one figure each from Units III and IV

UNIT VI

Unit VI Skill Performance Objectives

Swimmers should be able to perform the following skills for the designated times or in the designated way.

Strokes and Transitions:
Swimmer creates two different transitions.

Basic Positions and Sculls:
Inverted Vertical Position with Support Scull Hold—10 seconds

Inverted Split Rotation

Figures:
Kip

Eiffel Walk

Swordfish

Dolphin, Foot-First

Sequence:
Swimmer chooses her own music.

Transitions

In this unit the swimmer must create two transitions. She should remember that a transition is a movement from one body position or skill to another, or a movement which can be used to change direction in the pool. Swimmers should strive to create transitions which follow a logical progression, make movements look smooth, and avoid awkward body positions. Performing a transition well takes as much skill as performing any other synchronized swimming skill. When transitions are used in a sequence, they should appear as if they were meant to be written into the music.

Inverted Vertical Position With Support Scull Hold

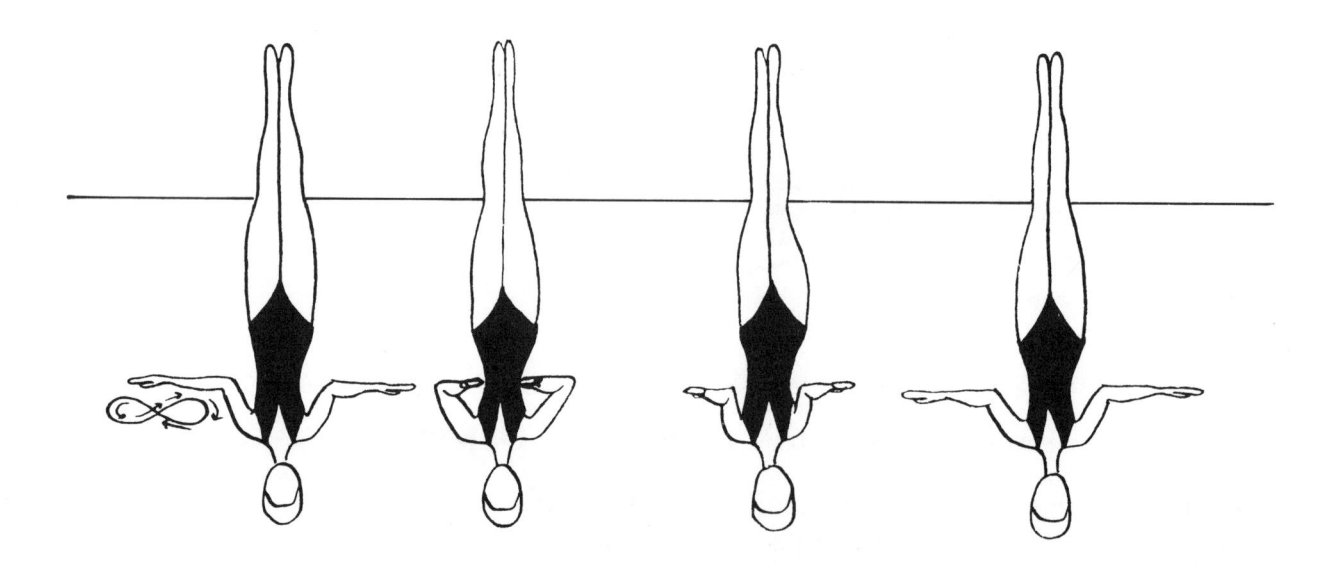

Method of Execution

The swimmer can get into the Inverted Vertical position in several ways: (a) She can perform a Porpoise by executing a Front Pike pull-down from a Front Layout and then lifting both legs; (b) she can assume an Inverted Vertical position while under the water and allow the body to rise to a controllable height as in a Barracuda; (c) she can execute a partial Back Tuck Somersault to a Vertical Tuck position and extend to an Inverted Vertical position; or (d) she can assume the position in any other way she can think of.

When a swimmer becomes proficient at this skill, she will want to obtain maximum height. However, it is easier to learn the skill if the body is allowed to assume its natural buoyancy level (usually about at the ankles). The swimmer should concentrate primarily on holding the position with the head, hips, and ankles in line, extended and perpendicular to the surface and on remaining stationary when learning it. This is not the time to work on getting height. As the swimmer's skill increases, the Inverted Vertical position should be performed with a waist level Support scull in order to achieve proper height.

Teaching Progression

On the Deck Have the Swimmers:

1. Stand against a wall and assume the correct posture by flattening the back against the wall, tucking the hips under, keeping the shoulders down and relaxed, the chin in, and the neck pressed against the wall. The head should be in line with the shoulders.

In the Water Have the Swimmers:

1. Assume an Inverted Vertical position by flattening their backs against the side of the pool while holding onto the gutter.
2. Assume an Inverted Vertical position by flattening their backs against the pool, hooking one knee over the side, and extending the other leg to a vertical position. The swimmers should help support the body by executing an overhead scull directly over the head with the elbows bent.
3. Assume an Inverted Vertical position by flattening their backs against the pool and having both legs extended vertically while a partner presses the swimmer against the side of the pool.
4. Practice the entire Inverted Vertical position in deep water.
5. Review the Support scull by standing on the bottom of the pool in deep water and maintaining the position on the bottom by sculling.
6. Review the Support scull by practicing the scull in a Front Layout position.
7. Practice the Inverted Vertical position with the Support scull.

Common Errors / Corrections

(See "Common Errors and Corrections" for the Support Scull, p. 82).

- Failure to keep the head in line with the body. Usually the head is back with the eyes focused on the bottom of the pool.
  - Point the top of the head to the bottom of the pool and look at the pool wall. If the swimmer is having a lot of problems with this, roll up a towel and have her grip it under her chin while executing the position.

- Arching the back.
  - Squeeze the buttocks, lift the rib cage, keep the shoulders down and relaxed. When the body is in a straight Vertical position, the swimmer usually feels as though the body is tilted toward the face or slightly piked.

- Piking.
  - Push the buttocks forward and roll the front of the thighs out. Stretch.

Common Errors (cont.)	Corrections (cont.)
• Falling to the side.	• Contract the muscles on the side of the body and push the legs to the side opposite the direction of the fall.
• Traveling.	• During an overhead scull, the hands must be directly over the crown of the head and the elbows must be bent. When using a Support scull, keep the elbows relatively close to the body.

Inverted Split Rotation

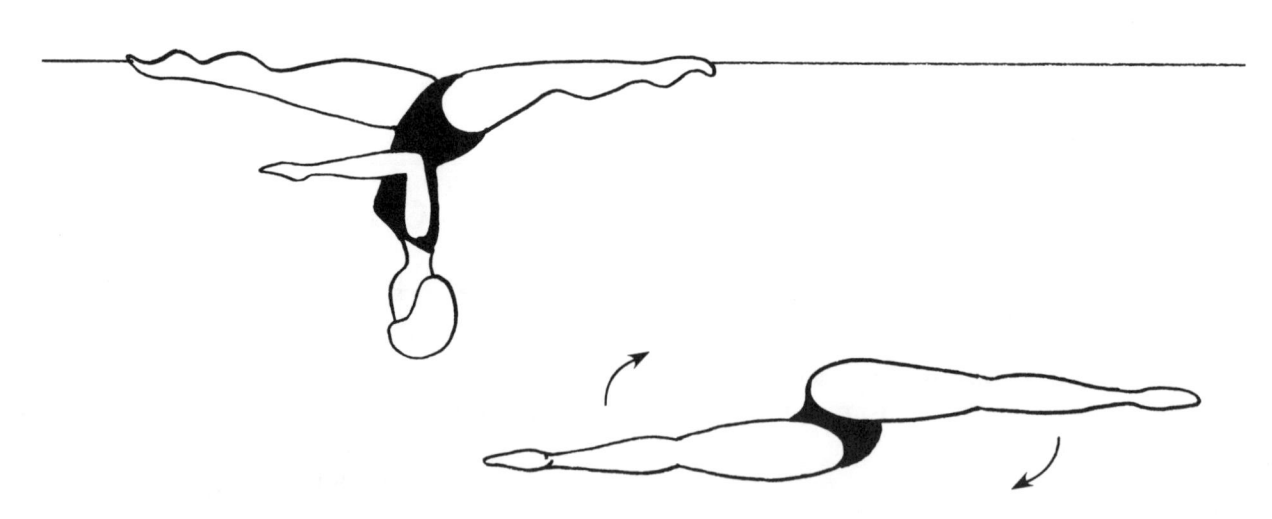

Overhead view of Inverted Split Rotation

Method of Execution

To perform the Inverted Split Rotation the swimmer first assumes a good Inverted Split position. The legs should be split evenly forward and backward, and both feet and hips should be as near the surface as possible. The torso is arched, with the shoulders under the hips and the head in line with the shoulders.

Once in the Inverted Split position, the swimmer places her hands directly over the crown of her head with the elbows bent and the palms facing the bottom of the pool. The arms and shoulders should be relaxed. The trick to turning is to "think turn." The swimmer will want to rotate slowly around an axis that runs perpendicular to the water and through the center of her trunk. The body must stay in a good Inverted Split position during the rotation. After the swimmer is more skilled, she should perform the rotation with her hands in the waist level Support scull.

Teaching Progression

Have the swimmers review the Inverted Split Position with Support Scull, pages 80-82.

In the Water Have the Swimmers:
1. Assume the Inverted Split position and have two partners each hold an ankle and turn the swimmer around the center axis of the body. Partners should think about keeping the swimmer in the correct Split position with the feet at the surface, helping the body stay balanced and the swimmer rotate.

Common Errors / Corrections

(See "Common Errors and Corrections" for the Inverted Split Position with Support Scull, p. 82.)

- Attempting to execute the rotation too rapidly which pulls the body out of alignment and creates an imbalance.
- Attempting to pull the body around in the rotation instead of sculling.

- Rotate slowly.

- Execute the correct scull.

Kip

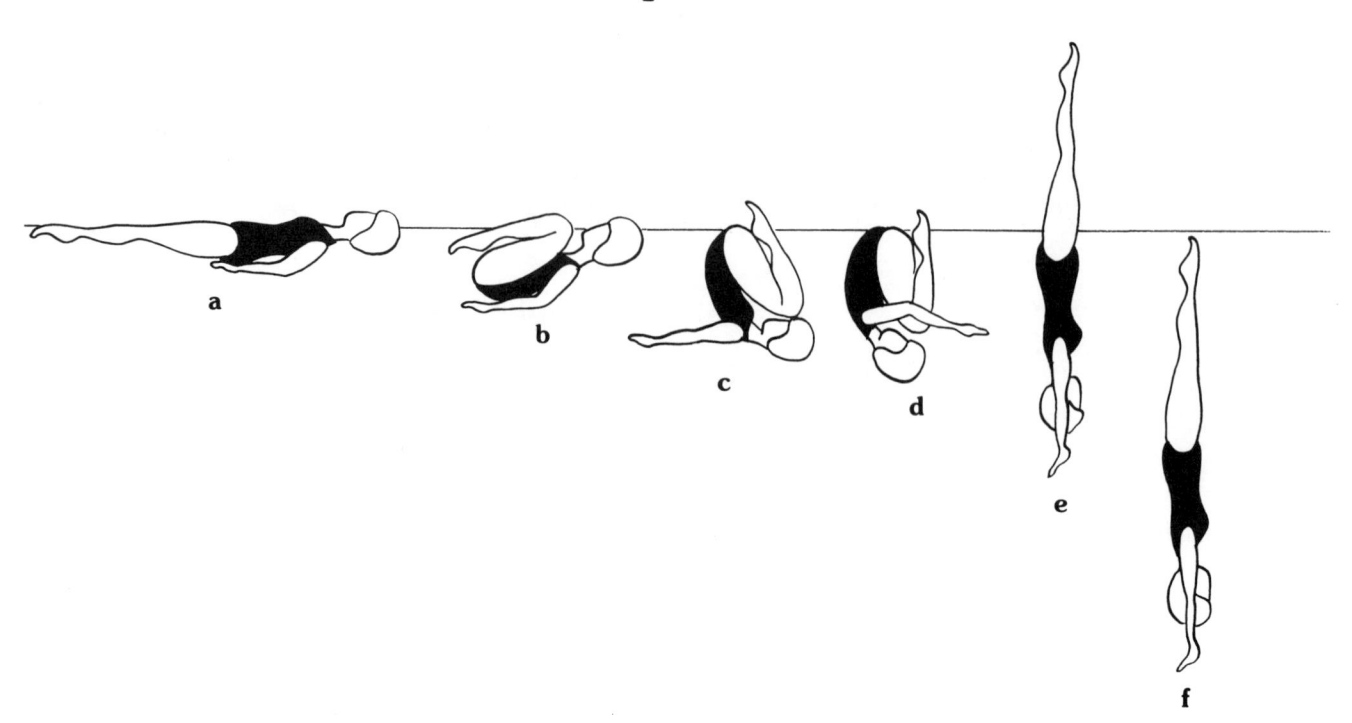

Method of Execution

The swimmer first assumes a Back Layout position. She then draws her knees to her chest, keeping her knees and toes at the surface, until she reaches a Tub position. Without stopping, the swimmer gets into a tight Tuck by pressing her head to her knees and her heels to her buttocks while executing a partial Back Tuck Somersault. The swimmer can use three possible arm actions to execute the partial Back Tuck Somersault:

1. She can move her hands level with the head with the palms facing the surface, pull through in small circular motions from overhead to the hips, and stop circling and start sculling when halfway over.

2. She can keep her hands at her hips with her palms facing the bottom of the pool, press down, and continue in a circular movement over her head. She should return her hands to her hips and start sculling when she is halfway over.

3. She can scull strongly behind her hips with her palms facing the bottom of the pool and the wrists sharply flexed, lift the hips, and press the body backward. When the partial roll is complete, she slides the hands forward close to her body with the fingers leading and sculls, keeping her hands close to her legs between the knees and ankles and the palms facing the bottom of the pool (see Figure d).

When the swimmer reaches the Vertical Tuck position with her shins perpendicular to the surface and her shoulders and back of the head facing the bottom of the pool, she stabilizes. She maintains the tight Tuck while performing a flat scull close to her ankles, parallel to and just beneath the surface. Her elbows should be close to the body, with the hands flat and in line with her forearms. While continuing to execute the scull in this manner, the swimmer extends her legs to a Vertical position by lifting the heels from the buttocks and knees from the chest in a fluid and continuous motion. The trunk, legs, and head should reach full extension all at the same time.

Once in the Inverted Vertical position, the swimmer should hold the position momentarily by performing a Support scull. Then she gently moves her arms to an overhead position and makes her descent. The descent is controlled by the overhead scull. The figure is complete after the swimmer's toes submerge.

Teaching Progression

On the Deck Have the Swimmers:

1. Assume a Back Layout position. They should move to a compact Tuck position and then slowly unroll the upper and lower body simultaneously to extend back into a Back Layout position.

In the Water Have the Swimmers:

1. Assume a Vertical Tuck position with their backs against the side of the pool and their hands holding onto the gutter. They should slowly unroll their bodies to an extended Inverted Vertical position.

2. Assume a Back Layout position. They should move to a compact Tuck position and then slowly unroll the upper and lower body simultaneously to extend back into a Back Layout position.

3. Practice the entire figure.

Common Errors

- Loose Tuck.

- Failure to roll to a true Vertical Tuck position.

- Loss of balance in the Vertical Tuck position.

- Throwing the head back and looking at the bottom of the pool as the body extends to a vertical position, causing the back to arch.

- Extending in sections instead of simultaneously. Frequently the knees are extended first, which results in a Front Pike position, and then the hips are extended by lifting the legs to a Vertical position.

Corrections

- Press the heels into the buttocks, knees into the chest, and nose to the knees.

- When the body is in the Vertical Tuck position, it usually feels as though it has rolled too far.

- Sculling should be close to the ankles, with the palms facing the bottom of the pool and the elbows bent and close to the body. Unnecessary body tension will make balance difficult.

- Keep the head in line with body. Point the top of the head to the pool bottom and keep the eyes focused on the pool wall.

- Extend the knees and hips simultaneously. Press the heels up and back.

Eiffel Walk

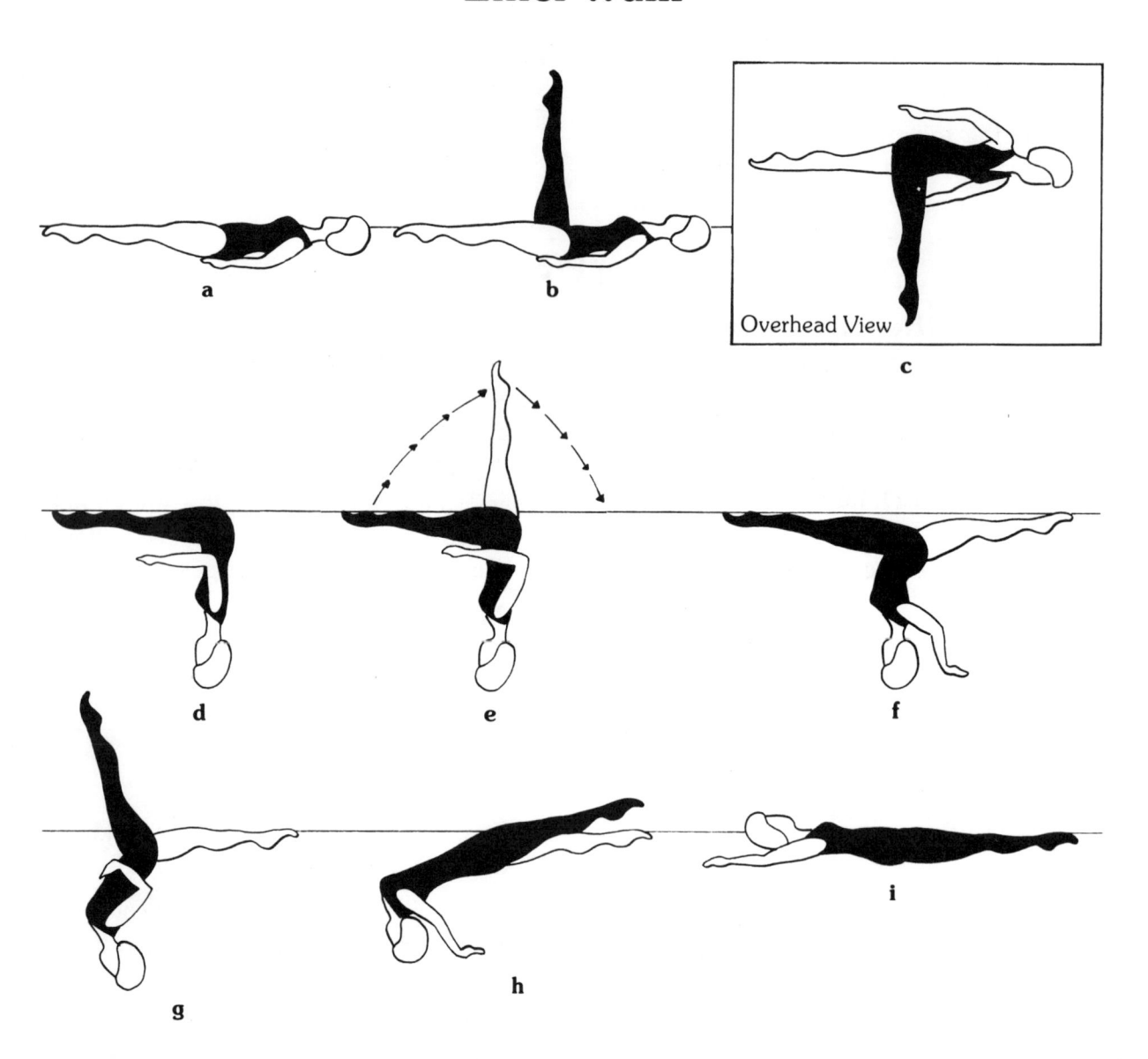

Method of Execution

In the Eiffel Walk, the swimmer executes a Ballet Leg and then transforms it into a Front Walkover. The swimmer starts in a Back Layout position and performs a Ballet Leg. Then she rotates around the horizontal axis running through her body, while locked in the Ballet Leg position, until her vertical leg is on the surface on the opposite side. Her head should stay in line with the trunk as it descends toward the water. The trunk remains straight and extended. As the body rotates, the left hand needs to execute a wider sculling motion and the right hand should continue to support behind the right hip. The legs should form a right angle throughout the rotation, and the foot of the extended leg should stay at the surface.

When the swimmer's vertical leg is on the surface, she is in an Eiffel position (see Figure c). From this position, the swimmer moves her trunk down into a Front Pike position while the leg which had been vertical moves across the surface to join the other leg. The swimmer should reach the Front Pike position at the same time that the feet meet. In order to assume the Pike, the left hand, with the palm toward the face, executes small sculls overhead. The right hand slips across the body overhead. The right hand slips across the body and sculls at the knees with the palm facing the pool bottom.

With the body in the Front Pike position, the hands should be at the knees, performing a flat scull with the palms facing the pool bottom. The swimmer then completes the figure by performing the rest of a Front Walkover. She lifts the leg which was in the horizontal position in the Ballet Leg in an arc over the surface to reach an Inverted Split position (see the Front Walkover, pp. 85-86).

The swimmer holds the Inverted Split position momentarily with a Support scull, then lifts the second leg in an arc to join the first leg. As the second leg passes the vertical, the trunk will be in a maximum arched position. As this leg completes the arc and joins the first leg, the swimmer moves her hands to a position over her head and finishes in a Back Layout. By performing a Reverse Torpedo scull, she won't move foot-first too much. The body should travel only enough so that the head finishes where the hips were in the Inverted Split.

Teaching Progression

Have the swimmers review the Single Ballet Leg (pp. 83-84) and the Front Walkover (pp. 85-86).

On the Deck Have the Swimmers:

1. Perform the Single Ballet Leg. They should lock in this position and rotate to the side opposite the vertical leg. Swimmers should concentrate on maintaining a right angle between the legs and keeping the body fully extended and aligned.

In the Water Have the Swimmers:

1. Perform a Single Ballet Leg with the horizontal leg supported on the pool gutter. The swimmers should rotate into the Eiffel position and continue into the Front Pike pull-down while moving the formerly vertical leg across the water to join the other leg on the gutter. Then they are to execute a Front Walkover, making sure to lift the leg which was horizontal in the Ballet Leg first in the Walkover.

2. Practice the entire figure away from the side of the pool.

Common Errors	Corrections
(See "Common Errors and Corrections" for the Ballet Leg, Single, p. 84, and the Walkover, Front, p. 86.)	
• Failure to roll the head and shoulders with the body to an Eiffel position as the Ballet Leg is rotated.	• The body must be locked into the Ballet Leg position and roll as a unit. The swimmer should watch the foot of the vertical leg.
• Failure to maintain the body in an extended position and completely aligned in the Eiffel position.	• Press the head and shoulders back. Do not press too hard on the heel of the horizontal leg or the back will arch.

Common Errors (cont.)

- Lifting the head to breathe while moving the leg from the Eiffel position to join the other leg.
- The leg sinks as it moves from the Eiffel position to join the other leg.
- Failure to reach the Front Pike position at the same time that the legs meet.

Corrections (cont.)

- Once the action is begun, the face must not be lifted from the water.
- Press the heel up and turn the knee down toward the pool bottom.
- Begin to move the trunk down as soon as the leg starts to move.

Swordfish

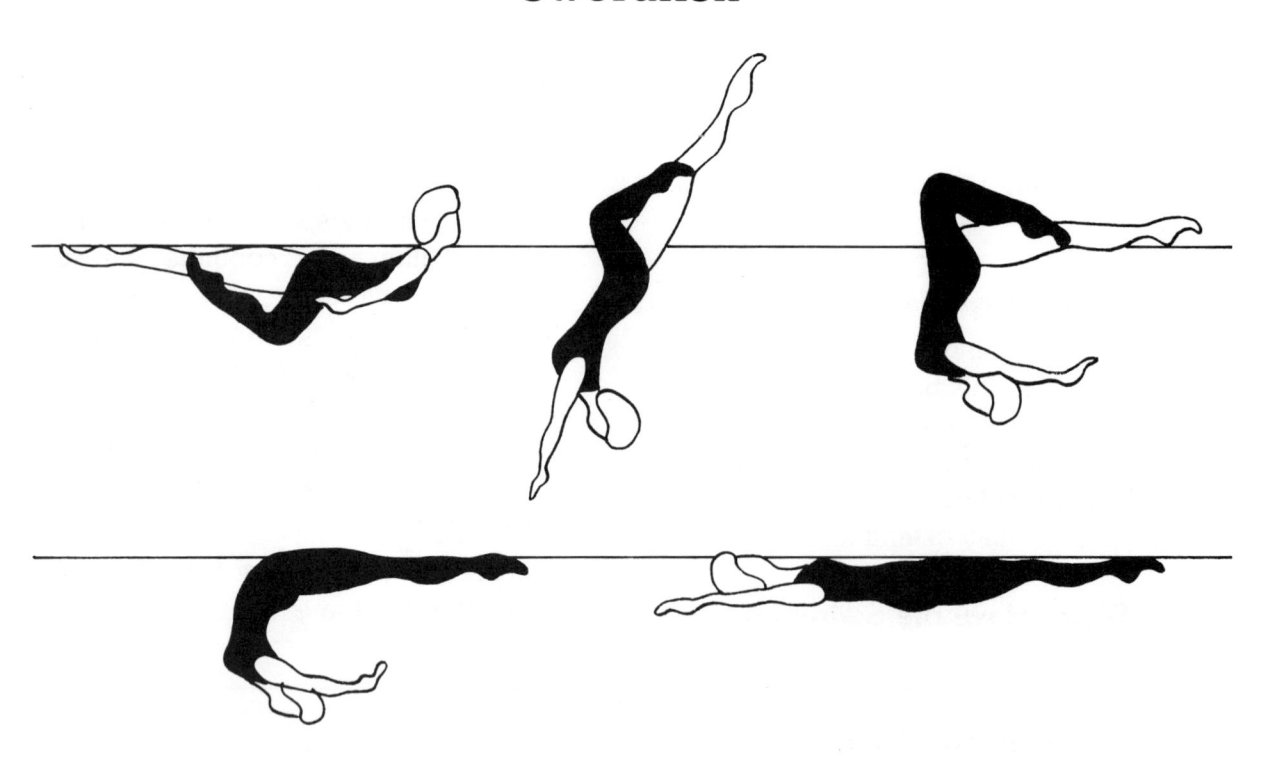

Method of Execution

To perform the Swordfish the swimmer first assumes a Front Layout position with her head up. She begins the figure by assuming a Bent Knee position while remaining in the Front Layout. To initiate the rotating movement, the swimmer lifts the heel of the extended leg and arches her lower back hard. While the leg is ascending, the swimmer can press her arms forward from the hips to the head, keeping her hands in line with her forearms, and while turning the hands sideways, slice the hands back to the hips with the little fingers leading. This motion is repeated as many times as necessary to get the leg over. Alternatively, the swimmer can use a "dog paddle" action with the arms by starting under the head and moving backward to the hips, first with one arm and then with the other. The hands should stay in line with the forearms. If the wrists hyperextend, the body will move in a foot-first direction.

As the extended leg moves in an arc over the surface, the body should pivot around an axis running through the hips. The body will be in a maximum arched position as the legs are gently lowered onto the surface. The swimmer continues sculling and extends the bent leg to join the other leg. The swimmer allows the body to surface and assumes a Back Layout position, finishing the figure with the head where the hips had been. By using a Reverse Torpedo scull, she can prevent the body from traveling too far.

Teaching Progression

In the Water Have the Swimmers:

1. Assume a Front Layout position with the head up and bend both knees, bringing both feet out of the water. While keeping their heads out of the water, the swimmers should arch their backs hard and scoop from the hips to the head until the body tips over to the back. Then they should unroll and Torpedo scull to the surface.

2. Assume a submerged arched position with both feet held on the pool gutter by a partner. They should keep their hips near the surface.

3. Practice the figure with a partner lifting the leg over in the arc.

4. Practice the entire figure.

Common Errors

- Piking at the beginning of the pull instead of arching.

- Body traveling foot first during the lift.

- Lack of height during the leg arc.

- Body sinking at the end of the leg arc.

- Excessive foot-first movement at the end of the leg arc.

Corrections

- Press the head back so it can be felt on the shoulders. Drape a small towel around the neck and hold it there with the head while executing the pull. Or, have a partner place a hand under the chin and lift it while the pull is executed.

- Make sure that there is a proper arch in the back and that the wrists are not hyperextended during the pull-over. Keep the hands in line with the forearms.

- May be caused by (a) lack of a proper arch, (b) lack of coordination between hip lift and arm action, (c) straightening the elbows during the pull, or (d) flexion of the wrists which pulls the body down.

- Lift up on the hips and bent knee toward the extended foot. Scull.

- Control with a Reverse Torpedo scull.

Dolphin, Foot-First

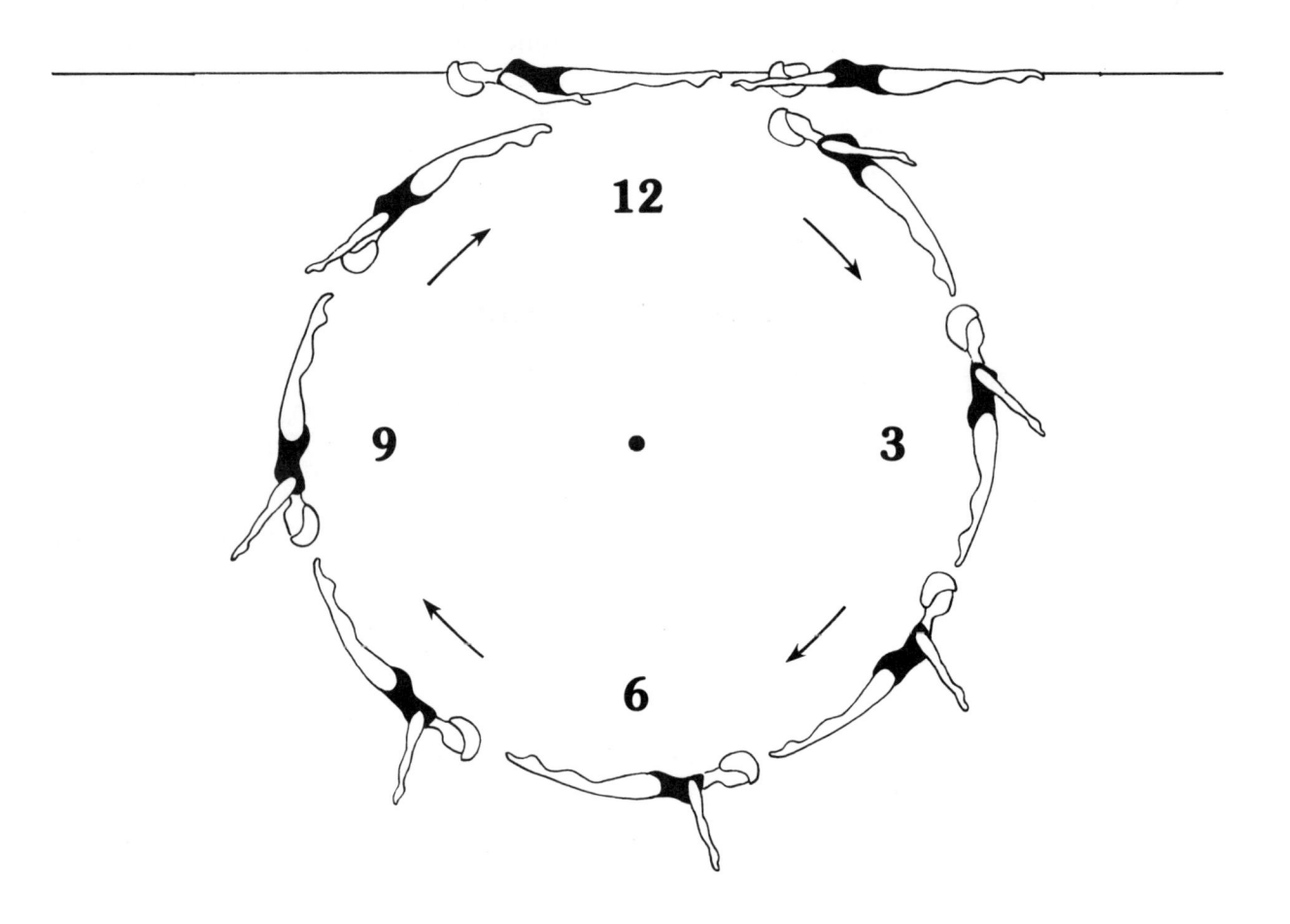

Method of Execution

In this figure the swimmer describes the same shape as in the Head-First Dolphin, but this time the movement around the circle is foot-first. The swimmer first assumes a Back Layout position and uses a Snail scull to initiate the foot-first movement. By arching her back and pressing down on her feet slightly, the swimmer submerges her legs, followed by her hips and lower back. The swimmer should continue to press on her heels to keep the slightly arched position.

As the chest submerges and the body assumes an arched Vertical position, the swimmer turns her palms to face the surface, bends her elbows, and extends her hands to her sides. She then scoops or pushes the water from her hips toward her head. After her hands are at her head, she slices them back to her hips, keeping them close to her body. This action is repeated as often as necessary to get the body to the bottom of the circle. As the swimmer's skill level increases, she should use a scull rather than scoops.

When the body begins to ascend to the top of the circle, the swimmer should bring her hands over her head. Because her natural buoyancy will cause her body to rise, the swimmer needs to use some reverse sculling to control the rate of the ascent.

The swimmer's toes should surface at the

same place at which they submerged. Once they come through the water, the swimmer presses up on the toes to keep them at the surface. The swimmer uses a scull to control the surfacing of the trunk and head. The swimmer should finish the figure in a Back Layout positon with the head in the same place at which the toes surfaced.

The circle which the swimmer describes is actually a process of arching and then straightening the lower back, and then arching and straightening the upper back. It takes four times through this process to complete the circle. The body is the least arched at the 3, 6 and 9 o'clock positions. Throughout the Dolphin, the swimmer must keep her body extended and slightly arched as in the Circle position described on page 12. The circle which her body follows should have a diameter one and a half times the swimmer's height, or about eight feet. During the Dolphin the swimmer's back should remain parallel to the horizontal axis around which she is rotating and her head, buttocks, and feet should stay on the imaginary line of the circle.

Teaching Progression

In the Water Have the Swimmers:

1. Assume a vertical, head-up position and execute a foot-first surface dive by scooping with straight arms from the hips to overhead, and then extend the arms straight out at the sides of the body. As the swimmers get close to the bottom of the pool, they should arch the lower back hard and transfer the straight arm pull from the sides of the body to in front of the body. They are to continue this motion until the body surfaces foot-first.

2. Assume a Front Layout position with their hands at their sides. The arms should turn out and pull from the hips to the head with the palms facing the head. Swimmers should keep the pulls even and smooth. Alternatively, they can use a Torpedo scull when they are more skilled and as the body descends transfer to the straight arm pull in front of the body.

3. Assume an Inverted Vertical position and begin a Torpedo scull while slightly arching the body. As the body surfaces, the swimmers need to gradually straighten the arch, beginning with the legs and following with the hips, back, chest, and head. They should finish in a Back Layout position.

4. Practice the entire figure.

Common Errors

- Turning sideways.

- Descending too vertically, cutting off the first half of the circle.

- Excessive foot-first movement before starting downward.

- Lifting the head off of the surface as the body descends to try to submerge the body.

Corrections

- Make sure to pull both arms evenly and not to roll the body to either side.

- Initiate foot-first movement before starting the descent.

- Press feet downward sooner.

- Keep the head in line with the shoulders.

Common Errors (cont.)

- Pivoting around the legs or the head instead of moving along the circumference, or moving the legs and buttocks along the circumference but not the head.

- Incorrectly shaped circle.

- Failure to resurface at the end.

- Feet popping out of the water at the end.

Corrections (cont.)

- Initiate foot-first movement before starting the descent and continue during the first quarter of the circle. Loosen the arch in the back.

- Review "Method of Execution."

- Reduce the arch in the lower back. Feel for air with the feet before allowing the head to ascend further.

- Arch the lower back more.

SEQUENCE 6

Swimmer chooses her own music

This exercise is the culmination of the Level I program. For this sequence the swimmer not only must choreograph her own routine, using the skills of this unit and the others, but select the music as well. When choosing music, a swimmer should think about what music will help her best present herself. She should be able to imagine herself performing fluidly and with variety to the music. The swimmer must remember that just because she enjoys listening to a song does not necessarily make it good music for a synchronized swimming routine. She should be willing to try something different and creative.

The sequence for this unit must contain all the skills learned in Unit VI as well as the swimmer's favorites from all the previous units. The swimmer should consider all the guidelines for choreographing a sequence that were presented in the other units, and above all, present her routine with confidence and stylish class.

APPENDICES

Appendix A: Scull Chart

Appendix B: National Achievement
                 Program Requirements

APPENDIX A

SCULL CHART

Scull	Body Position	Hand Position	Wrists	Direction of Movement
Eel	supine	at hips	hyperextended flat	head-first stationary
Snail	supine	at hips	flexed	foot-first
Canoe	prone	at hips	hyperextended flat	head-first stationary
Alligator	prone	overhead	flexed	head-first
Torpedo	supine	overhead	hyperextended	foot-first
Reverse Torpedo	supine	overhead	flexed	head-first
Lobster	prone	overhead	hyperextended	foot-first
Support	vertical	at hips	flat	stationary

APPENDIX B

National Achievement Program Requirements

United States Synchronized Swimming has developed a National Achievement Program to help swimmers assess their progress. The six steps in the Level I program correspond to the six units in this manual. As swimmers learn the skills in each unit, they can take the test which corresponds to that unit. For each test, the swimmer must be able to perform all but one of the skills taught in that unit, plus the sequence. If she passes the test, she will receive the National Achievement patch award for that unit and can start working on the skills in the next unit. The patch is in recognition of the swimmer's accomplishments and hard work.

The requirements for each of the tests are listed below, along with a picture of the patch awarded when the swimmer passes.

Unit I

Do seven of the following eight skills, plus Sequence 1.

- Side Stroke—25 yards
- Crawl Stroke—25 yards
- Eel Scull—15 yards
- Snail Scull—15 yards
- Tub—One each way
- Somersault, Back Tuck
- Oyster
- Water Wheel—One each way

Unit II

Do eight of the following nine skills, plus Sequence 2.

- Back Stroke—25 yards
- Breast Stroke—25 yards
- Canoe Scull—15 yards
- Alligator Scull—15 yards
- Torpedo Scull—15 yards
- Corkscrew—One each direction
- Log Roll—One each direction
- Somersault, Front Pike
- Jumpover

Unit III

Do seven of the following eight skills, plus Sequence 3.

- Side Flutter Kick and one variation—25 yards
- Reverse Torpedo Scull—15 yards
- Bent Knee Position Scull, Supine—10 yards each leg
- Bent Knee Position Scull, Prone—10 yards each leg
- Shark Circle—One each direction
- Marlin—One each direction
- Somersault, Back Pike
- Dolphin, Head-First

Unit IV

Do seven of the following eight skills, plus Sequence 4.

- Eggbeater Kick, Stationary—30 seconds
- Lobster Scull—15 yards
- Vertical Tuck Position
- Inverted Split Position with Support Scull
- Ballet Leg, Single or Alternate
- Walkover, Front
- Dolphin, Bent Knee
- Porpoise

Unit V

Do six of the following seven skills, plus Sequence 5.

- Eggbeater Kick, Traveling—15 yards
- Flamingo Position
- Crane Position
- Ballet Leg Submarine, Single
- Somersub
- Walkover, Back
- Barracuda

Unit VI

Do six of the following seven skills, plus Sequence 6.

- Two transitions created by the swimmer
- Inverted Vertical Position with Support Scull Hold—10 seconds
- Inverted Split Rotation
- Kip
- Eiffel Walk
- Swordfish
- Dolphin, Foot-First

BIBLIOGRAPHY

American Red Cross. (1981). *Swimming and aquatic safety*. Washington, DC: Author.

Counsilman, J.E. (1977). *Competitive swimming manual*. Bloomington, IN: Counsilman Co.

Counsilman, J.E. (1968). *The science of swimming*. Englewood Cliffs, NJ: Prentice-Hall.

Horn, B. (1974). *Swimming techniques in pictures: Expert instruction*. New York: Grosset & Dunlap.

Jones, F.L., & Lindeman, J.I. (1975). *The components of synchronized swimming*. Englewood Cliffs, NJ: Prentice-Hall.

Lundholm, J.K., & Ruggieri, M.J. (1976). *Introduction to Synchronized Swimming*. Minneapolis: Burgess.

Martens, R., Christina, R.W., Harvey, J.S., Jr., & Sharkey, B.J. (1980). *Coaching young athletes*. Champaign, IL: Human Kinetics.

Reeves, M.A. (1974, December). Basic sculling. *Synchro-Info*.

Roberts, S. (1980). *Star manual*. Ottawa: Canadian Amateur Synchronized Swimming Association.

Thomas, D.G. (1972, June). Universal sculling. *Synchro-Info*.